Stop:
LIVING
YOUR JOB

Start
LIVING YOUR LIFE

Stop
LIVING
YOUR JOB

Start
LIVING YOUR LIFE

85 Simple Strategies to Achieve Work/Life Balance

ANDREA MOLLOY

Ulysses Press

Acknowledgements

Thank you once again to friends and family who have supported me during the writing process—you know who you are!

Also a big thank you to Jenny Hellen, Karen Ferns, Michelle Hurley and Sarah Thornton.

Published by ULYSSES PRESS
       P.O. Box 3440
       Berkeley, CA 94703
       www.ulyssespress.com

First published in 2004 as *Get A Life!* by Random House New Zealand

Library of Congress Catalog Control Number 2004110116
ISBN 1-56975-453-5

Printed in Canada by Transcontinental Printing

10 9 8 7 6 5 4 3 2 1

Cover design: Lourdes Robles-Aragón
Cover image: ©Barton Stabler/gettyimages
Text layout: Katy Yiakmis
Editorial: Leona Benten, Lily Chou, Claire Chun, Lisa Kester

Distributed in the United States by Publishers Group West
and in Canada by Raincoast Books

Contents

Introduction

The balancing act

Happiness is the meaning and purpose of life.

— ARISTOTLE

Do you often feel swamped by emails, piles of paperwork, meetings, unpaid bills and increasing demands on your home and work life? Most of us are so busy these days that we rarely take time out to stop and evaluate our lives honestly. We all have aspirations, but daily hassles can slow our progress and even bring our dreams to a total stand-still. We are left feeling that there has to be more to life than commuting, working long hours, studying, juggling childcare and struggling to organize our personal lives.

Few of us currently have the balance we are striving for in our lives. It is not uncommon for people to ask themselves: "Is balance even something that I can achieve?" There is a prevalent myth regarding the elusive work/life balance—that we can have and do it all. Let's get this straight: it is physically impossible to single-handedly be a full-time parent, work 100 hours per week in a high-profile career, study full time and be a professional athlete. While the last two decades have encouraged us to "have it all," we are not superheroes and we need to prioritize what we truly value in life.

There is no easy answer or quick fix to the question of balance. If you feel that your responsibilities are controlling you, or you just want to enhance your ability to live life to the full, learning how to take charge of your life is a good place to start. You have to work at it, however, and not simply rely on workplace policies to present a balanced life to you on a platter.

We are all experiencing a much faster pace at work, driven by technology, downsizing, competition and a move away from the expectation of a "job for life." Outside of work, single-parent households are on the rise, there are many more families in which both parents are working, and our overall life expectancy has been extended. There is a real need for everyone to address the integration of their work and home lives.

Balance is much more than dividing time between separate compartments of our lives. Success or failure in any one part of your life will naturally impact on the quality of other parts of your life. For example, stress at home will often overflow into your working life, impacting on your ability to do your job.

So what exactly is work/life balance? Put simply, it is a sense of control, achievement and enjoyment in everyday life. The challenge when seeking balance is that we all have our own interpretation of how a balanced life will look. Whether you envisage yourself as a full-time homemaker, working part time, traveling or operating three businesses, achieving balance requires constant attention to avoid conflict between the different areas of life. It is this conflict that so often leads us to feel we are constantly frazzled and "running out of time."

In the workplace, balanced work/life practices have

benefits for both organizations and individuals. Research now shows conclusively that in companies where employees are able to achieve a balance between their working and home lives the staff are more productive, stay in their jobs longer, have reduced absenteeism, have an increased return rate from parental leave, experience less stress-related illness and record higher morale and commitment to the company. Ultimately, in a business sense this means bottom-line results.

A recent Mt. Eliza Business School study showed that Australasian managers consider work/life balance to be their number one challenge for the future. This is now beginning to be seen as a broad issue that affects individuals, families and workplaces alike. In my own research, survey respondents have told me that the biggest challenges of work/life balance include time management (39%), being organized (16%), financial pressures (10%), lack of energy (9%), emotional management (9%), childcare (7.5%), saying "No" (7%) and living with a work-focused partner (2.5%). On an individual basis, integrating work and life adds value to our daily lives, reducing stress and improving relationships in all areas of life.

While increasing numbers of companies and organizations are starting to focus on offering "family-friendly" policies and "work/life integration," *Stop Living Your Job, Start Living Your Life* addresses what you can start doing right now to make a difference. It will increase your awareness of how to balance your work, relationships, family, friendships, fitness, contribution to the community, study, recreation and "me time."

This book isn't just for the stereotypical happily married couple with 2.5 children. The traditional nuclear family is not the only sector of society that is struggling to balance the demands of their lives. Whether we are single, living with a partner, married, divorced or widowed, we are all experiencing increased demands such as looking after elderly parents, study, workplace pressures and juggling our social lives. One person's experience isn't any more significant than another's. Regardless of where you are in your life cycle, if you are feeling increasingly overwhelmed by the demands you face, the simple strategies outlined in *Stop Living Your Job, Start Living Your Life* will help you learn to live a balanced life.

In my first book, *Aspirations: 8 Easy Steps to Coach Yourself to Success* (Random House, 2003), I presented a step-by-step program for building a successful life. Let's briefly recap on the process:

Step 1—set effective goals in every area of your life

Step 2—align your goals to your personal values

Step 3—take the best care of yourself

Step 4—simplify your daily life by "working smarter, not harder"

Step 5—overcome your limiting beliefs

Step 6—boost your confidence

Step 7—develop strong communication skills

Step 8—maximize your motivation.

I was overwhelmed with positive feedback from my first book, and many readers of *Aspirations* asked specifically for more strategies and practical tips on balancing home and work. This has resulted in the book you are now reading. For those who enjoyed *Aspirations*, I have again taken a practical and common-sense approach in presenting a wide range of useful strategies. I have used real-life case studies (with changed names) and anecdotes from survey respondents to illustrate how applicable these strategies are. My aim is for you to increase your awareness, focus on your priorities, take responsibility, make the best decisions in your life and always take action.

Many of the concepts and strategies introduced in *Stop Living Your Job, Start Living Your Life* have been tested in my own life or are based on the success stories of clients. In researching this book, I have also consulted focus groups and surveyed hundreds of people. Once again, I return to my role as a personal coach who facilitates others' development. In no way am I prescribing a specific way to live, but I am presenting a number of options to allow you to individually make the choices that will best assist you.

How to use this book

Throughout the book I encourage you to make positive changes in your life, step by step, by applying the strategies I discuss. Be inspired by the concepts and continually focus on how you can implement each of them in your own situation.

Each chapter can be read independently. You may feel that some are less relevant to your situation than others—make sure you still read these sections, rather than ignoring them and hoping that your life will improve regardless! You might consider reading a chapter each week, every two weeks or each month, and then start using some of the strategies. I recommend that you buddy up with friends who are facing similar issues of work/life balance. By establishing your own *Stop Living Your Job, Start Living Your Life* motivational group (see Chapter 1) you can continue to discuss and share ideas that work, and together learn to live the ideal lives you desire.

As we explore work/life balance you will need to ask yourself some challenging questions about your values and attitudes. Answer these questions honestly, because the information you gain from this process will benefit you only if you are totally truthful. So, as you read each strategy, keep in mind that you are in the driver's seat and have control over the future direction of your life. Remember too that a strategy that is perfect for one person may not be ideal for you. Customize the strategies so they apply most effectively to your particular life.

In **Chapter 1**, I show you how to step back from your hurried daily life and ponder the "big picture." This will help you discover your purpose and your key priorities in life by increasing your self-awareness. I look at creative ways in which you can uncover your potential and refocus your aspirations. I also explore ways you can gather your personal support team around you to keep you on track and moving forward in your life. Balancing your life is impossible unless you appreciate how your aspirations can be realized while honoring your responsibilities and commitments.

Chapter 2 provides you with numerous strategies so you can instantly organize your life, make better use of your time and increase your personal efficiency. Each and every one of these strategies can make a real impact on your work/life balance. They will make a real difference to how you run your daily life, ultimately creating more time and space for you to focus on your priorities.

Chapter 3 addresses stress—not just how to identify stress in our increasingly busy daily lives, but how to manage it in the longer term for a healthy, fulfilling life. The reality of modern living is that everyone experiences stress in some way at some time. Once you understand stress and how it appears in your life you can choose to reduce your stress levels, which will bring you closer to balance. All the health experts I spoke to while researching this book agreed that managing stress is best achieved by living a healthy lifestyle—eating well, exercising regularly and relaxing. In this chapter I show you easy ways to make lasting changes to your fitness schedule and nutrition habits to help provide a foundation for your work/life balance plan.

Chapter 4 takes a closer look at techniques that you can use to connect your mind and body to achieve work/life balance. Visualization, meditation, affirmations and intuition may sound New Age, but they have very practical uses that will show real results as you strive for balance. You may decide to use some of these strategies to reach your aspirations or for relaxation, both of which will assist you as you work toward work/life balance.

Chapter 5 shows you how to maximize your motivation, beat procrastination and get going. You may have the best plans and intentions for work/life balance, but this chapter shows you how to transform your life to the next level. In it I introduce strategies for encouraging you to keep on taking action and show you how to make sustainable changes. There are tips on taking the first step, continually improving, being consistent, staying committed and celebrating success.

Throughout the book you will see icons that indicate where you can get more involved:

Quick quiz: These quizzes are an ideal way to raise your awareness and provide areas for improvement or development in your life. They are not complicated tests, simply a starting point for self-awareness, allowing you to identify where you can focus your energy to make changes.

Action task: Have a notebook handy as you read the book so you can complete action tasks as they appear. Completing each action task will help you to translate the concepts, ideas and strategies into workable solutions that suit you personally.

Action question: *Throughout the book you will notice short questions in italics. These action questions are something you can take away and ponder, contemplating your own answers to inspire change.*

What looms ahead may seem overwhelming, so take the time to complete this quick self-assessment quiz to evaluate where you are now. Increasing your self-awareness is a pivotal first step in moving toward work/life balance.

Quick quiz: Is your life in balance? Answer "Agree" or "Disagree" to each statement, then check your score. There are no right or wrong answers—the most important thing is to be absolutely honest so that you can identify your needs and goals and move forward.

1. I enjoy my work and feel fulfilled with my life purpose.
2. I am clear on my personal priorities and know what is most significant to me in life.
3. I have a strong network of family and friends who support me.
4. I spend rewarding time with my family and friends.
5. I have financial goals and long-term plans for my security.
6. I have a realistic schedule that allows me to focus on my priorities.
7. I use technology to my advantage in helping me plan my day.
8. I have effective systems in place to manage paperwork, projects and bills.
9. I am aware of my financial situation and use a practical budget.
10. I am engaged in work that enables me to balance my life in other areas.
11. I am assertive and know what I want to say "Yes" to.
12. I regularly unwind and create time to relax.
13. I choose to eat mostly low-fat, fresh foods.
14. I am active in my daily life and feel rejuvenated by regular exercise.
15. I fall asleep easily at the end of the day and wake feeling refreshed.
16. I watch my attitude and think positively.
17. I use positive self-talk to achieve my goals for work/life balance.
18. I believe in my ability to reach my aspirations while retaining a healthy balance in life.

19. I can imagine what my new and improved ideal life will look like.
20. I always use positive, empowering words when I communicate with others.
21. I am flexible and readily adapt to change.
22. I very rarely procrastinate on important tasks.
23. I often take stock of challenges and resolve to overcome any potential obstacles.
24. I always reach goals I have set out to achieve.
25. I am fully responsible for my choices and actions.

Score: If you found that you disagree with any of statements 1–5 you might not be as fulfilled as you would like. Read the strategies in Chapter 1 to help you focus your life as a whole and discover your personal priorities.

If you disagreed with any of statements 6–10 you might choose to adopt some of the personal organization strategies in Chapter 2.

If you answered "disagree" to any of statements 11–15 you might need to concentrate on managing stress and building a healthy lifestyle, as outlined in Chapter 3.

If you disagreed with any of statements 16–20 you will benefit from the mind-body strategies in Chapter 4, which highlight the importance of self-belief and positive attitude.

Finally, if you disagreed with any of statements 21–25, boost your achievements with strategies from Chapter 5. Remember that work/life balance is an ongoing process, so you might want to revisit this chapter in the future to boost your enthusiasm.

Chapter 1

Get focused

I've learned you can't have everything and do everything at the same time. Tell yourself the truth about what matters most to you.

— OPRAH WINFREY

Achieving balance in life does not mean a 50% allocation of time between work and family life. There will always be times of natural focus as you manage work deadlines, study for exams, or perhaps care for an ill relative or child. Life is fluid and work/life balance is a dynamic process. The balance also changes dramatically as you progress through your life cycle—as you have children, for example, enter a long-term partnership, start a new career or head into retirement.

While our lives are mostly consumed with work, family and a range of "must do" everyday tasks, this chapter will help you focus on the reasons behind why you work so hard. Rather than living your own version of *Groundhog Day* (remember the movie!), take the time to become focused on what matters most to you. The strategies that are discussed in this chapter will help you focus on your big-picture dreams, concentrate on your priorities, build a strong support network and look at the importance your financial life plays in the balance game.

Focus on your dreams

A generation ago most of us would have faced the societal expectation of a job for life, owning a home in suburbia and being part of a traditional nuclear family. Now, many of us dream of changing careers, traveling and turning our hobbies into businesses. We might aspire to own a vacation home, or simply take a vacation! Regardless of your position, you need to—as they say in management speak—get a "helicopter view." This will help you to put your life in perspective. Then you can begin to revisit those hidden dreams and passions that will make you feel truly alive. When you have identified your passions you can narrow your focus, set compelling goals to reach your dreams and achieve balance.

Action task: Spend some quiet time thinking, writing in your journal (more on journal writing in Chapter 4) or contemplating your answer to the famous coaching question: "If you could do anything in life and knew you simply could not fail, what would you do?"

Think big

So, if you could do anything in life, what would *you* do? Just imagine—if the sky was the limit, you answered to no one, money was no object—how would you spend your life? To create changes and balance in your life, first you need to be clear on what you want in the broadest sense.

If you feel overwhelmed imagining your wildest dreams, start by asking yourself why you are reading this book. Let me guess—you want to be more organized, have more time, reduce stress, increase your fitness, earn more and work smarter, not harder? Very admirable, but dig a little deeper and think about why you want these things. What is the higher goal or big dream that motivates and drives you? Let yourself dream of the possibilities, and promise not to get bogged down by the finer details and potential obstacles.

If you are having difficulty defining your big-picture goals, stop and think! Visualize your life 10 years from now—and remember you really do have the internal resources to know what your big dreams are. Imagine your life when it is balanced just as you want it. Even if you have not totally identified your big dream, you probably know the general direction in which you want to head. While I am not saying that you will achieve your dreams in picture-perfect detail, it is important to get a feeling for the type of life you want to lead. We can't predict the future, so our big-picture dreams show us what is most important and where to focus our time and energy.

Big dreams might seem wildly improbable now, but don't write them off just yet. Looking back on my own "dreams list," jotted down in the diaries of my teenage years, I see that I had listed writing a book (this is my second and I have a third in mind!) and traveling to the U.S. to see my favorite rock band, Aerosmith, live in concert (something I did recently to celebrate my 30th birthday). The message here is: don't discount your greatest aspirations. You might surprise yourself when you connect with your dreams and, more importantly, put yourself in a position to actively look for opportunities to make them happen.

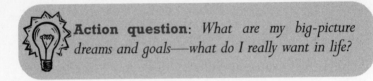
To get started on formulating your dreams, ask yourself these questions:

- Imagine yourself on your 99th birthday, then ask what you will recall as highlights, successes and accomplishments in life?
- If a writer was researching a biography on your life, what would you want included as your achievements?
- As a child, what did you always imagine you were going to be when you grew up?
- In your ideal life, where and how would you live? How would you spend your vacation? What sort of lifestyle would you lead? What would you do for work?
- If you didn't care what people thought of you and were guaranteed to succeed, what would you do . . .?

 Action task: To help you to think big, create a dream list. Daydream and let your mind float into the future. Then compile a list of special dreams.

Find your passion

Passion is a word that implies a strong emotional desire. When you see or read interviews with high achievers, you will notice they always refer to this elusive factor as a driving force behind their accomplishments. Passion arouses you to take action since it creates a sense of urgency—it is what excites you and makes you feel truly alive. To find your passion, next time you feel a burst of energy or a natural high, stop and focus on what grabbed your attention—it is likely to be an unrealized passion. Remember, your passion is not always what you get paid to do. While you may be lucky enough to have a career that you are passionate about, your passion may be something else, like a sport, some form of art or your involvement in charity work.

Remember that living a passion-filled life is not dependent on your skill level (how good you are at the activity) but how engaging you find it—whether it is playing the violin, books, cars, gardening, photography, extreme sports or being a volunteer firefighter.

At some point, most people tell me they don't know what they want—but relax, because part of you really does know. Recently a client who attended one of my seminars looked at me blankly when I asked if she knew what her passion was. Cheryl was a 42-year-old mother of three with a heavy workload as an accountant for a global company. During the previous three years, all her spare time had been consumed by studying for an MBA. I gently asked her, if she had an afternoon to spend how she liked, what would she do? She replied that that was an easy question since she loved music, and would write and sing new songs. It was a moment of inspiration for Cheryl as her passion was glaringly obvious, but she hadn't acknowledged its importance in her life. Cheryl had no immediate intention of leaving her secure career to embark on a life as a pop star, but she knew that to feel fulfilled in life she needed to spark her passion by writing music.

Finding your passion may take a little longer than five minutes, but it will happen. Of course, if you have forgotten what you love to do it will be harder to identify your passion, but more on that later.

Shortly before starting to write this book I worked with Jen (34) whose core goal, like many of my clients, was simply to discover her passion so she could regain balance in her life. She took an interesting approach by committing to a year-long "passion project." As an experiment, she read books on subjects that wouldn't normally interest her, surfed the Internet, went to shows, concerts, seminars and interest groups, and took up classes in everything from cooking, writing, art and music to pottery, dancing and languages. She was able to experience a diverse range of activities that she had not previously encountered, with a view to uncovering her hidden passion. She also reconnected with hobbies she had enjoyed earlier in life but had since become too busy to spend time on. Fortunately, Jen was financially able to work on her "passion project" full time, but I have since had many other clients adapt this idea by taking a range of low-cost night courses to broaden their horizons in search of their hidden passion.

Action task: Spend an afternoon browsing in your local bookstore or library, or surfing the Internet. What subjects or categories are you intuitively drawn to? Or, each month try a new hobby, interest or activity. Note your experiences in a journal and describe what inspires you so that you can identify any patterns that point to your hidden passion.

Notice what you love, then list at least five things that make you feel alive—consider sports, hobbies, friends, family and recreation.

Passion appears in our lives in varying ways, but a common theme many of my clients have noted is realizing that a passion for something makes you feel energized and confident when you are doing it. Another good indicator of a passion is the anticipation and excitement it generates. You may also lose track of time when you are caught up in living your passion. So indulge your passion, whatever it is—if you love golf, fishing or dancing, devote special time to it.

Magazine editor and novelist Nicky Pellegrino found her passion at an early age and now balances a full-time job with up to four hours a day of writing.

"Writing is the only thing I've ever shown the remotest talent for. I've always loved it, ever since I was a child and wrote my first poem, called 'I wish I had a pony,'" she explains.

Journalism was a natural career choice for Nicky, but she always believed she would write fiction too.

"I love to read novels and, like a lot of people, my ambition was to write one myself and have it published," she says.

Describing her daily routine when she was writing her first novel, *Delicious*, Nicky comments, "It didn't feel like 'work' because I loved doing it. I would wake up at 7 a.m. and walk my dog for an hour and think about my plot and characters. Then I'd get home, scribble a few notes and get myself off to work. At night I'd get home and pick up on the stuff I'd been thinking about that morning and start writing."

Nicky is the first to admit that during this time demands on her life increased.

"Some things I let slide. I ate a lot of takeout and my house didn't get cleaned as often. My social life took a dive, and for a while my husband didn't see much of me."

To stay focused and balanced, it became important for Nicky to ride her horse and dig in her vegetable patch. She describes these as good de-stressors, plus they can count as exercise.

While being positive, Nicky likes to keep her accomplishments in perspective.

"While hundreds of thousands of people have written novels, I'm glad to be one of them at last. I still feel I have a long way to go—more novels to write, more things to do," she says of her passion for writing.

Some self-coaching questions to discover your passion:

- In the past, what interests have captured your attention?
- If you could choose absolutely anything, what would you spend most of your time doing?
- If you were following your passion, how would life be different from your current life?
- What are your strengths and talents?
- What have you relegated to the "I'll do it someday" pile?
- I was always meant to be . . . ?
- Choose five alternative careers or imaginary lives.

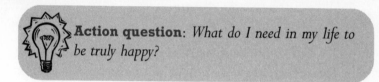

Create your vision

If you have ever worked in a corporate organization you will probably be familiar with the idea of a company vision. One well-known company is famous for its vision of a computer in every home. However, very few of us apply the idea of having a vision to our own lives. In fact, creating a vision is very effective because it creates a buzz of excitement around your dreams. It is also the first step to making them a reality.

When I asked you to think big, you may have started instinctively to create your personal vision for life. The idea is to take the big dreams and decide which to pursue to create your vision for the future. This will probably include relationships, family, social life, career, education, "me time," health, fitness, recreation and leisure. Write a description of how each aspect would look in your ideal life. Alternatively, if you are a visual person, make a collage or scrapbook, cutting pictures from magazines and newspapers that symbolize your vision for life.

The purpose of creating a vision is to clarify what your version of work/life balance and success will look like in your life. If your vision matches your current life — excellent, you are well on your way. However, most of us have yet to reach our potential. Remember, you are much more likely to follow through with your action plan when you have a very clear picture of exactly what success and balance look like for you.

Turn the dream into reality

It's fun to fantasize about your future, but you also need to plan an action strategy. The easiest way to turn your dreams into reality and achieve life balance is to set compelling goals that show commitment to your vision. Effective goal-setting is the first step toward realizing your aspirations. In effect, what you are doing is breaking down your big-picture vision into manageable, "bite-sized" pieces that you can act on.

Put simply, goals are future-based targets that will guide you to your ideal life as they cement your intentions. If goal-setting appears tedious, keep in mind that goals enable you to make your life vision a day-to-day reality. There's no denying that dreams are realized through good old-fashioned action.

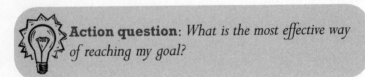 **Action question**: *What is the most effective way of reaching my goal?*

Goal-setting tips:
- Write down your goals—even buy a new journal in which to record your goals and track your progress.
- Use positive language when setting goals.
- Assess your goals against the SMART rule: goals need to be Specific, Measurable, Achievable/attractive, Realistic and Timed to a deadline.
- Set short-term goals to achieve within the next three months and longer-term goals for six

Get a Life

months or longer.

- Break down your goals into manageable segments or "action tasks."
- Focus on two or three goals at a time. Don't overload yourself with 30 different goals and achieve none.
- Regularly evaluate and track your progress, adopting new options for a way forward where necessary (see Chapter 5 for additional strategies).

Action task: Revisit the big-picture ideas created using the previous three strategies. Focus your dreams into key areas. List the top 10 things you want to add or improve in life to achieve work/life balance. Now take a fresh piece of paper or open your journal and set SMART goals in each area of your life that you want to develop, such as career, education, finance, health/fitness, family, relationships, leisure.

Prioritize your goals

Once people have identified their big dreams and set compelling goals, many wonder what to do next. Working alongside individual clients, I spend a substantial amount of time helping them to prioritize their goals for the next three, six or twelve months, or longer. Some of your goals may order themselves naturally. For example, if you are working toward an overseas vacation, you will need to achieve a debt-reduction goal first, to enable you to access money to travel. Similarly, if you want to restructure your working hours, you may need to first meet relationship goals that allow you to discuss your current financial and working situations with your partner.

Using a theme will help you focus on what is your high-
est priority for the immediate future. It will help you to make
sense of your big-picture vision, and also give an overall
sense of direction to your specific goals. It will remind you
to prioritize your day-to-day activities to honor your theme.

I often ask clients to create a theme for a six- to twelve-
month period by asking them to finish this sentence in their
own words: "2005 is the year of . . ." For example, if you are
starting a new business venture, your theme could be as
simple as "start-up," or if you are recovering from an illness,
"self-care" might sum up your theme and bring together
specific health, fitness and well-being goals. Other themes
clients have used recently include "fun and adventure,"
"romance" and "balance."

Action task: Prioritize your personal goals by
writing down all your dreams, desires and aspirations. You may have 30, 50 or more items detailed.
Review your list and highlight your top five items—those that
you are prepared to put the most time and effort into achieving.

Now, revisit your goals and give the next six months or
year a theme. Check in with yourself and ask what is the
single most important thing that you could achieve in your
life right now? The idea is to have an overall theme that
brings together your core goals for work/life balance rather

than having an ad hoc approach for the coming months. Use your theme to keep focused on what is important to you at this time, and use it to say "No" assertively when you are being drawn away from your priorities. Having a vision and a theme are useless unless they are backed up with an action plan and a "how to" strategy.

Focus on your priorities

We have all heard the saying that no one on their deathbed ever wished they had spent more time in the office. Another that I heard recently is "Work won't make you coffee in the morning," referring to the importance of family and friends in our lives. By focusing on your priorities, you will automatically make room for what matters most to you.

To be honest, I find clients often make dramatic life changes following a break-up, job loss, illness or close family death. Sometimes these events can be catalysts to re-evaluate life. Time and time again, those who have recovered from a major illness or accident tell me they have a fresh perspective on life. Don't wait to be in a life-threatening situation before you evaluate your priorities in life.

In addressing your work/life balance, you first need to identify what issues you are facing at your particular stage in the life cycle. It could be balancing a job search, managing your workload, studying, gaining a promotion, raising a new baby, facing childcare issues, organizing your home life, maintaining your social life, planning for retirement, traveling, staying healthy, giving quality time to your family or any number of other issues. Once you have been through this identification process you can actively honor your priorities.

Every day we are also faced with issues that question our priorities. Do you work late or go home? Do you get a second job to get out of debt, even if it means time away from your family? Do you stay in your job or retrain for a new career? Do you become a stay-at-home parent or return to work? All these questions force us to make decisions about our priorities that in turn reflect our values. Here we will look at how you can define your purpose and clarify your values so you can focus on your priorities.

Discover your purpose

If you can answer the question "Why am I here?" you have already uncovered your purpose. Like your passion, your purpose is much deeper than simply choosing a satisfying career. It is about adding meaning to your life—perhaps identifying your mission, vocation or calling. This doesn't mean that everyone will be volunteering for overseas aid work or joining a religious order. Your purpose will most definitely reflect your values (as discussed in the next strategy) and it will also mirror your personal vision and give your life overall direction. Having a purpose is bigger than the daily hassles of life. It is the reason you live and value your own life. Ask yourself, what gives my life meaning? Start by noting down the most meaningful experiences in your life so far and identifying why they were meaningful. Just as you earlier wrote down your vision and theme, again I am asking you to take quality time to focus on your purpose. The reason for these self-directed exercises is to continually increase your awareness of who you are and what you want in life. It would be frivolous to write just one page of thoughts in 20 minutes then change your life accordingly. This way, your responses to several action tasks will begin to show trends in your personal wants and needs.

I regularly ask clients to write their life purpose in a sentence, mostly for their own clarity and sense of life direction. Here are a few guidelines:

- Think of verbs (doing or action words) that describe your purpose. Examples include create, direct, communicate, sell and teach.
- Use nouns to describe who or what your purpose relates to. Does your purpose relate to children, friends or customers, for example?
- Include an outcome you are striving for and your strengths or talents.

Here is an example of a purpose sentence from 45-year-old Greg: "My life purpose is to . . . build and strengthen families using my counseling skills, to help adults to be better parents."

This is 51-year-old Jill's purpose: "My life purpose is to . . . create a loving family environment that nurtures and supports my children's development as independent, well-adjusted individuals."

Action task: Spend some time contemplating how you want to express who you are in your lifetime. Using the guidelines outlined in this strategy, complete this sentence: "My life purpose is to . . ."

Live your values

Create your life in a way that is consistent with the values you hold. This may sound like a vague, New Age concept, but put simply, values are your personal priorities. In his book *Finding True North*, Michael Henderson succinctly defines values as the sum of your preferences and priorities. Identify your personal values and use them as a reference point in your everyday life. So what are your values?

Here is a list of some values to get you started:

achievement	adventure	arts
authority	autonomy	career
community	creativity	environment
family	health	honesty
independence	integrity	leadership
learning	loyalty	money
privacy	recognition	relationships
religion	security	service
status	travel	

Action task: Review the values listed in this strategy and compile your own list of personal priorities. Then list your top 10 values in order of importance. Remember not to censor yourself—values are exclusively yours, so focus on what is significant in your life.

Explore the gap between what you deeply value and the reality of your daily life. Check that your goals and behavior are aligned to your values. For example, if you rate health as your number one value, yet you smoke, drink excessively and don't exercise, you are out of balance. If honesty is one of your core values but your work requires you to sell a product you don't believe in, you will find this imbalance will impact your entire life. By making a reality check on your values you are highlighting areas for action to bring these values into alignment.

If you find that your values are in conflict you need to decide which value has greater importance to you. This isn't just something to do on paper—use real examples to test competing values. For example, if family is of higher value to you than friends, you might decide to turn down a social invitation and instead help your daughter with her homework. Do you work on your art (value: meaningful work) or spend time with your wife (value: family/relation-ship)? Do you renovate your house (value: home) or do you put the money toward your children's education (value: family)? Again, there is no right answer, only *your* answer.

Another fun way of testing that you are honoring your values in everyday life is the front-page test. Imagine that whatever decision you are about to make is going to be reported on the front page of a national newspaper or, even better, on the TV news. Will you be proud to be associated with the news report and have no regrets about your behavior? A resounding "Yes" means you are honoring your values and priorities.

 Action question: *What do I need to add or remove from my life to bring it into alignment with my values?*

I actually have a list of priorities, with my husband and family being the most important, and work being lower down the list. This makes most decisions in life easy to make. For example, if friends ask me out but I haven't had a date with my husband in a while, I choose time with my husband.

— JANE, 26, SPORTS COORDINATOR

Find work you love

Regardless of whether or not you get paid to work at your passion, you should enjoy your work and find it stimulating. While there are many reasons for working, including the challenge, sense of contribution, achievement, status, respect and sense of community, most people I have spoken with say that ultimately they need the money they earn to support their families and themselves. This is a fair comment, but the right job for you will not only showcase your strengths and talents, and provide you with an income, it will help you achieve better all-around balance throughout your life.

If you have lost the buzz that work used to give you, look to establish a special project at work—something you can concentrate and focus your energy on to revive the interest you once had. Alternatively, if you love your job but don't like the company you work for, maybe it is time to leave and find a new employer. I admit this is easier said than done, so I would first recommend that you take stock of what is missing so you know what you need to be satisfied. Once you have an idea of what is needed to boost your enthusiasm, you can set effective goals to make the needed changes before finding another company to work for.

Many of my personal clients who are in career transition choose to generate a criteria system. It is a simple and useful idea that you can also apply to your choice of work. While your criteria system will reflect your personal values, it also allows you to consider the practicalities of your working life. Consider the importance of the location of your work, size of the company, work hours, bonus package, salary and training. Damian, a 26-year-old market analyst and father of two, included in his criteria that work should be less than a 30-minute drive (in rush hour!) from home, and he required an employer contribution to medical insurance. He didn't rate highly whether it was a company of five or 500 people, or whether the job was based downtown or in an industrial park. When he was looking for a new position, he was able to focus on the responsibilities of the role, knowing he had a benchmark for specific criteria that must be met before he would accept an offer. Damian, like most who use this concept, found this a reassuring way of gaining work/life balance, as it took into account the most important factors based on his particular lifestyle.

Action task: List your own job criteria so you can increase your chances of finding work that you love. Check the differences between your new criteria and your existing job, and commit to taking action to make positive changes.

> *My main priority is to make sure that I'm okay financially. Everything else follows from this. I do make sure though that everything I do to bring in money centers around my passions.*
> — CHERYL, 29, EDITOR

Focus on people

Building your own "dream team" is vital in providing enthusiastic encouragement as you work toward balance in your life. Most of us think we can reach our goals and "do it all" independently. The reality is that our lives are highly dependent on others. Just as work, home, time and money are interlinked in our lives, so are other people. Our ability to succeed is very dependent on the quality of our relationships with others and the support they give.

Elite athletes and teams rely on their supporters at events and games to reach their potential as well, of course, as their managers and coaches. Boost your morale by increasing your support team too. The following strategies highlight several ways in which you can gather practical and useful support.

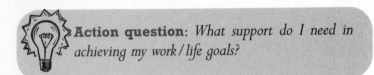

Action question: *What support do I need in achieving my work/life goals?*

Build a strong network of family and friends

Undoubtedly, friends and family will fill the fundamental role of being your support team. Think about the people in your life today—friends, family members, more distant relatives and work colleagues. Identify those who already inspire you and challenge you to meet your goals and balance your life. Who really fires you up when you discuss your ambitions? Is there anyone else you can think of who might be able to assist you? Look for people who can help you to achieve your goals and who you already turn to, especially during events such as illness, job layoff, death, divorce or a family tragedy—a good indicator of a person who truly does care.

Be upfront and honest about asking loved ones for their support—they will usually be delighted to help. Describe exactly what you want to achieve, and specifically how they can help. This is a key point, as so often people ask for generic support and are disappointed when their expectations are not met. It may be stating the obvious, but don't expect your support team to be mind-readers— clear communication is crucial.

Ask your support team for their opinions too. For example, "If you were setting this goal, what ideas would you have for achieving it?" More importantly, listen to their ideas and adopt those you think are most appropriate. In Chapter 5, I will show you how to seek valuable feedback from your support team.

Be aware that while you might expect close family and friends to be pleased that you are making improvements in your life, some may feel undermined or even prefer the status quo. Learn how to handle their negativity by remaining positive and determined to succeed.

Reality check: do you have enough positive, supportive people in your life? If your answer is "No," consider what steps you are prepared to take to increase your support network. You may need to start by widening your social circle, which will enable you to consciously meet like-minded people. Begin by considering those close to you who you haven't previously approached for support.

Stretch your comfort zone and ask for the encouragement you need. In return, of course, be receptive when you are approached by others seeking support. Continually nurture your relationships with small gestures like a thank you note or calling a friend just to say "hi."

Aside from friends and family, also identify profess-ional support—the people on the periphery of your life who you could potentially enlist as you move forward in your life:

drycleaner	nanny	personal trainer
gardener	housekeeper	nutritionist
financial advisor	mentor	event/party planner
masseuse	stylist	image consultant
travel agent	voice coach	personal coach
admin services	accountant	lawyer

Don't be afraid to hire help or consider bartering ser-vices with friends and neighbors. The aim is to put support systems in place to free you up to focus on your priorities.

Action task: Identify the personality characteristics and attributes you feel are important for your support team. List the best people to include in your support group. Schedule and plan how you are going to get them involved.

Look to role models

Learning from role models is another straightforward strategy. Your role model could be someone you admire, identify with and learn from. It might be someone you know personally, like a colleague, or someone you don't know, like a high-profile celebrity or businessperson such as Oprah Winfrey or Donald Trump. If you are finding it difficult to identify a role model, read books and magazines that feature inspiring interviews with "can do" people, or watch documentaries featuring those who have overcome incredible obstacles.

The great thing about role models is that to have reached their level of success and gained your admiration, they will have needed enthusiasm and passion for their own dreams. Examine what they have done to keep their life balanced as they achieved their dreams, and think about how you can emulate their success. Chapter 4 features visualization techniques using role models, which expands on this idea.

Action task: Identify your role models and ask yourself what it is you admire about them, how they inspire you, and which of their qualities you would like to adopt.

Use a mentor

I am often asked, "What exactly is a mentor and how do I use one?" In short, a mentor is someone who has been there, done that. The word is Greek in origin, and means a trusted advisor. A mentor will generally guide and teach using their own experience as a basis. Often a mentor will pass on short cuts and tricks of the trade, but more importantly they will share challenges and obstacles they have had to overcome in their own journey. These will often include issues surrounding work/life balance.

Contemplate who you would like to consult as a mentor. When you have approached your ideal mentor, consider a time when you can meet regularly. Depending on your priorities, you might choose different mentors for various areas of your life. For example, an entrepreneur might choose a separate mentor for marketing and business planning. You might choose one mentor for career goals and another for a community project you are working on. Meanwhile, a new manager might approach an established and respected CEO for leadership mentoring.

This kind of relationship requires strong commitment on your part, as mentors often donate their time. Before you say, "The person I want to mentor me is sure to say no," let me reassure you that very rarely do I hear stories of refusal. If you choose your mentor carefully, they will usually be flattered that you value their experience and will enjoy the process of guiding you to your goals. Being a mentor is both rewarding and satisfying; while you might not choose to work with a mentor, perhaps you have the skills and experience to consider mentoring someone else.

Mentor checklist:
- What type of mentor would best meet my requirements?
- What do I want to learn or understand?
- Who are my ideal mentors?
- How can I find a potential mentor?
- How can I approach a potential mentor?
- How do I plan to work with my mentor?

Start coaching

Coaching is an excellent way to increase your awareness of any work/life balance issues, and to progress toward your ideal life. Just as athletes and sports teams have coaches to help them train and reach their physical goals, you can use coaching to further your own potential. A personal coach facilitates, encourages and motivates you to set and reach effective goals. During regular sessions, your coach will guide you as you resolve challenges, overcome obstacles, consider options, adopt creative solutions, maintain focus, implement strategies and evaluate your outcomes.

Coach yourself

If you are particularly ambitious and driven you can coach yourself on work/life balance with excellent results. In *Aspirations* I introduced the GROW model, which is a simple coaching model anyone can use. This model was popularized by Sir John Whitmore in *Coaching for Performance*, and it is the basis for many styles of coaching.

- G is for turning your issue into a Goal.
- R is for giving yourself a Reality check.
- O is for considering all your Options to move forward.
- W is for committing to a Way forward and taking action.

Using the GROW model, here are some coaching-style questions that you can use to coach yourself or a friend in a co-coaching relationship:

Establishing a GOAL:
- What is the issue or what is wrong?

- What do I want to achieve?
- How do I imagine the situation when it is resolved?
- What measure can I use to show I have achieved the goal?
- When do I want to have achieved this goal?

Exploring REALITY:
- What is happening now?
- What is missing?
- What have I done so far to improve things?
- What obstacles or barriers are stopping me from moving forward?

Considering your OPTIONS:
- What steps can I take toward this goal?
- Brainstorm at least six options to choose from.
- What are the pros and cons of each option?
- If the sky was the limit, what would I do?
- What else could I do?

Finding your WAY forward:
- Which options will I commit to as action steps to move closer to the goal?
- When am I going to start and complete each action?
- Is there anything else I need to consider?
- Do I need additional support?

Co-coaching
Co-coaching has an advantage over self-coaching, as many of us naturally increase our accountability and support

levels by working with someone else. It is a great option if you have already tried coaching yourself and lost momentum. Consider co-coaching a close friend or work colleague. As with self-coaching, use the GROW model to provide structure to your sessions. Before you start, set some ground rules to avoid potential misunderstandings:

- Agree to hold either in-person or phone sessions weekly.
- Confirm the length of each session (typically 45–60 minutes).
- Commit to the length of your partnership (up to three months).
- Commit to confidentiality by drawing up a contract.
- Start each session with a report on progress since your last meeting.
- Spend equal time on each person; for example, take a turn each week to work through your goals.
- Remember the golden rules of coaching—do not give advice, and use open-ended, effective questions to elicit answers.
- Continually focus on solutions and not past problems.
- At the end of each session, write notes agreeing to the discussed goals and commitment to actions.

While the GROW model sounds great as a theory, here is a quick, simplified example of it in action between two people:

Coach: *"What goal would you like to work on today?"*

Coachee: "I want to get a new job."

"What makes you want a new job?" (Reality checking.)

"It's too stressful where I am, and I always have to work late so I can't pick up the kids."

"What would you like in a new job?"

"That's easy—more flexibility so I can start early and finish early, which would fit around my family better and reduce my family pressures."

"OK, so what you are saying is that you don't necessarily want a new job, but you need more flexibility. What exactly are you looking for, since we need to make this a SMART goal?" (Determining the goal.)

"Ideally, starting at 9 a.m. and finishing at 3 p.m. every day. I think a month is a fair enough time-frame to have this sorted out."

"To recap, your goal is to work from 9 a.m. till 3 p.m. Monday to Friday, starting within one month?"

"Yes—it's amazing; before our session I was sure I had to leave my job, when in reality there are other options."

"So, let's look at some of the options available to you to achieve your flexible working life."

"I could still get a new part-time job with these hours. But looking at my current job, which I really do like, I can talk to my manager about reduced hours, talk to the HR department to see if they have any flexible working policies, see if anyone wants to job share, maybe work from home or even become a contractor for total flexibility."

"What option will you commit to doing before our next session?"

"Given that I like my job, I think I'll start by talking with the HR manager in case there are any policies in place that I can take advantage of. I'll talk to her on Monday morning. Then I'll talk with my manager once I have information from HR."

This example shows how the process flows in a natural conversation. The key is that the coach mostly listens, and asks very few questions. I can be in session with a client for 45 minutes and ask just six or eight effective questions. This way the coachee or client is drawing on themselves as a resource.

Hire a coach

Nothing beats having a professional coach of your own to help you set and achieve goals—OK, so I am biased, but with good reason! Professional coaches are experienced in using advanced listening, effective questioning and coaching concepts in order to facilitate your development. The coaching process is fully focused on you as a client, enabling you to achieve the best results. As a client, partnering one-on-one with a coach, you choose the areas you want to work on, such as career, education, finances, health, fitness, family and relationships. Your coach will support you 100% and, unlike friends and family, coaches are non-judgmental and thoroughly objective. This provides a solid structure for accountability and momentum.

If you choose to hire a coach, start by checking that they are a member of the International Coach Federation— this is an independent professional body that establishes ethics and sets codes of conduct for coaches. In addition, check that they have reputable specific training as a coach, and ask for client testimonials. Remember too that while formal experience and qualifications are very important, you will be working with your coach on your biggest dreams and aspirations, so make sure you get along with them. Building a strong rapport with your coach is fundamental.

Expect to work with your coach for three months. Like fitness training, this is a short enough time-frame to keep you focused and motivated, but long enough that you are able to achieve your goals and complete specific projects. Whether you meet in person or use a coach via phone, commit to hour-long weekly sessions to build momentum and accountability.

Create your own *Stop Living Your Job, Start Living Your Life* motivational group

In his 1937 self-help classic *Think and Grow Rich*, Napoleon Hill coined the phrase "creating a mastermind of people around you." The idea here is to bring together a small group of achievement-oriented people with differing talents, skills and backgrounds to help you brainstorm ideas and provide suggestions on how you can reach your goals. The group also provides peer accountability, and is an excellent forum in which to evaluate your progress.

Establishing a *Stop Living Your Job, Start Living Your Life* motivational group is not an excuse for gossiping over a cup of coffee; it is an opportunity to benefit from fresh perspectives in a supportive, confidential environment. I recommend you partner with like-minded friends who are also facing work/life balance issues. By establishing your own *Stop Living Your Job, Start Living Your Life* group you can discuss ideas that work, and together learn to live the ideal lives you desire. While some people find taking the first step toward achieving personal goals challenging, more often it is keeping up the momentum and taking the second and third steps that throw us off course. A *Stop Living Your Job, Start Living Your Life* group is an ideal way to boost your enthusiasm and keep you committed.

In establishing a *Stop Living Your Job, Start Living Your Life* motivational group use these guidelines:

- Approach six to eight like-minded people from differing professions (this provides variety); for example, a lawyer, marketer, banker, builder, entrepreneur, journalist, property developer and IT specialist.
- Agree on a plan for how you can support each other. Consider how regularly you can meet, when and where? Agree to meet at least once or twice a month for an hour.
- Set ground rules for your group meetings, including confidentiality, constructive feedback and non-judgmental support.
- Ensure you have a clear structure to your meetings so everyone has the opportunity to discuss their issues and goals, brainstorm ideas and report on their progress.
- Alternatively, you might choose to work through each chapter of this book. Start your meeting by discussing how a particular section relates to you, and identify the areas in which each of you wants to specifically set developmental goals to improve your work/life balance.
- Commit publicly in your group to specific actions so that the next time you meet you can review your progress.
- Remember to use the advice of others appropriately. Consider the opinions of your support team and motivational group, but make up your own mind.

Network formally

Networking is the art of socializing, but it can also be a valuable vehicle for meeting like-minded people who share similar goals and can support each other. It can also be the perfect way to identify your role models or even meet a potential mentor. Many professions have their own networking organizations, such as accountants, coaches, engineers, human resources advisors, lawyers, managers, marketers or small-business owners. There are also specialist networking groups for women and other groups. Formal networking raises mutual issues and often involves lobbying or policy making. More informal groups like book clubs, writers' workshops and parent groups are primarily interest- or lifestyle-based, but they too provide an opportunity to connect with others who are experiencing similar issues to yours.

Networking tips:
- If you are nervous about meeting people, take a deep breath before entering the room.
- Greet people with a firm, confident handshake.
- Introduce yourself with a snappy, genuine 30-second introduction.
- Ask questions—people love to talk about themselves, and you will learn more about them.
- Hone your small talk by testing your own conversation starters. Know hot topics, even current affairs.
- Have business cards easily accessible for exchange. Don't force your card on others;

start the process by asking for theirs—this also shows that you are interested in them.

■ Body language and your style leave lasting impressions. Maintain eye contact, listen and smile!

Focus on financial freedom

Are you in debt most months? Do you regularly go into the red before your paycheck is due? Is money always at the back of your mind as the pressure builds? Or do you budget diligently, know when your credit-card debt will be paid off and save for your retirement?

Did you know that sex and money are the most common reasons for relationship breakdown? The role of money is not surprising, given that it is such an emotionally charged area of our lives. There is simply no denying that money is the major means of exchange, and that it can influence our lifestyle in a number of ways. In focus groups that I have facilitated, people regularly tell me how important money is; in today's society it is primarily what we use to pay for our basic needs—shelter, food and clothing. Often this is why our work becomes a top priority in our lives, especially if it is the main source of family income.

> *Work comes first as it's important to earn an income to have a life.*
> — MICHELLE, 31, ACCOUNTANT

The term "financial freedom" is often bandied around by gurus, who use it to describe the situation of no longer having to work a nine-to-five day as your investments work for you and provide ample income. However, "financial freedom" does not have to mean that you are fully self-sufficient; not everyone aspires to such a high level of freedom, which usually entails large sacrifices along the way. Financial freedom may simply mean the security of knowing you will be well looked after in your retirement years, or it may mean having enough money to take regular overseas vacations. Financial freedom, financial security or financial independence—choose whichever term fits your values and goals. I use them interchangeably in this section.

The first lesson is that you do not need to be a top earner, receive an inheritance or win a lottery to become financially independent. Do the numbers, figure out the type of life you want to live and, as a result, what you need to do now to be able to live that way.

In speaking with clients about financial freedom the key point I keep hearing is that they need to learn to manage money so that they can stop worrying about it. Many people tell me they would like to be in a situation where they have enough money saved and invested, or enough income streams, that they don't have to work for a living. They might choose to work when they want to, and on their own terms, but it should not be a necessity.

If you are reading this and thinking I sound crazy, when you are overextended on a mortgage, trying to cope with crippling interest from a credit card and seem to be forever paying for something, don't turn the page in a huff. Read on, because you do need to get a serious grip on your finances so you can achieve the balance that is required to live the life of your dreams.

The best piece of advice I have received recently is that money is just a tool. The way you handle money can tell you a lot about yourself. In this section we will revisit goal-setting and how it applies to your finances, change your beliefs about money, find opportunities for creating passive income, and think long term. Each is an important strategy in your quest for work/life balance.

Pursue your dreams

Earlier I invited you to think big, create a vision and pursue your dreams. I am assuming that some of your goals involve finances. If not, let's look at the money issue from another perspective—how many of your goals will need financial resources to make them a reality?

Action task: It's a fantasy most of us consider at some point: imagine winning $20 million in a lottery. What would you do with that amount of money? Write down every dream and desire you can think of—have fun with this game. When you have listed everything you can think of, review your list and see how many items you really want. From your list pick the top five or ten items. If you won't be satisfied in life until you have seen the Pyramids of Giza in Egypt or owned a beach house, start planning for it now, rather than regretting in 20 years that you never created the opportunity to actually make it happen.

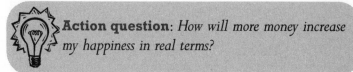

Action question: *How will more money increase my happiness in real terms?*

Set financial goals and make a plan

Generally clients tell me that they want more money—it's a key financial goal for most of us. You don't need to be a financial wizard to realize that there are two ways to acquire more money—earn more and spend less!

Forget about "get-rich-quick" schemes and "buy now, pay later" bargains. Financial freedom all comes down to planning and goal-setting. Use the same principles as you would for your career or relationship, introduced earlier in this chapter. Having specific financial goals will increase your motivation levels too. People regularly tell me how much easier it is to save money when they are working toward a vacation, or a down payment on a house. If you are aware that you operate in this way, continue to set goals that relate to your financial resources. Setting financial goals will not turn you into a money-hungry monster—it's a sensible, mature approach to life. I would even go so far as to say that if you are going to set goals in only one area of your life, choose to set financial goals, then let your new goals flow from your better position.

If you have put planning for a secure financial future at the bottom of your "to do" list, now is your chance to make some positive changes. It's never too late to take control and set financial goals. In my early 20s, I was highly irresponsible with my finances, living from paycheck to paycheck, despite a generous income. While I set goals for my fitness and career, my financial situation didn't even appear on my radar. I was hoping that if I ignored it, the situation would go away—big mistake! Believing there was plenty of time to start saving, invest or plan for retirement, I spent money without any thought and my student loan and credit card debt spiralled out of control. To get back on track I have had to make major adjustments to my lifestyle. The key benefit is the sense of security that has developed as my finances have improved and I have reduced the stress of worrying about whether or not I can pay my rent next week or buy groceries. I am also more relaxed knowing that I am taken care of financially if life throws a curve ball at me. Many of my friends are facing similar issues as they return from extended periods of travel with mounting student loans, to become part of the "sandwich generation," entering long-term relationships and starting families in their 30s. In the future, as this generation faces retirement, they will find themselves sandwiched between children just entering college while they also support elderly parents. But more on long-term planning later—let's start with prioritized financial goals for the next three to six months.

Sanjay, a 23-year-old science graduate, realized that while he was starting his career he had to make some hard choices about his financial goals. He wanted to plan for his retirement, save for a down payment on a home, pay off his student loan, replace his car and buy a home entertainment system, but with a limited graduate salary he couldn't do it all at once. Like most goals, his financial choices needed to be prioritized and compromises made, especially if he was to achieve a balance between his wants and needs. If you find yourself in a similar situation, faced with a number of conflicting options, check in with your values to decide what is most important for you. It may seem obvious to pay off the student loan first, then save for the next goal, but how many of us actually do this? How many of us are living our financial dreams?

Common areas for setting financial goals include implementing a budget, reducing debt, paying off student loans, establishing a three- to six-month emergency fund, buying a house, funding care for elderly parents, generating passive income, planning for retirement and investing. You may be considering home renovations, a wedding, starting a family or a dream vacation. Be wary of financial goals that are centered around spending money rather than making it! Remember, once you have decided on your financial goals, you need to turn them into effective SMART goals, as discussed earlier in this chapter.

Spend some time writing a financial plan to keep track of your longer-term financial goals. Susanna Stuart, a senior financial advisor at PricewaterhouseCoopers and author of *Your Family Fortune*, says, "Having a financial plan is like having a road map or an architect's plan designed to help you achieve your goals."

A financial plan is not just a budget (see Chapter 2). Typically your financial plan will include:

- Debt-reduction plans
- Savings and investments
- Retirement planning
- Asset protection
- Tax planning
- Daily money management (bank accounts, installment-plan purchases and credit card use—this is also known as cash management, and it includes your budget).

In your planning phase, take a closer look at your investments (properties, shares, business) and how they are performing. If you don't have any investments, develop a strategy and start saving. Include in your financial plan protection for your assets (e.g. your home, car, boat) and appropriate insurances.

Change your beliefs about money

In *Aspirations*, I introduced the idea of self-limiting beliefs—the negative beliefs that hold you back and serve as obstacles that stop you moving forward in life. As Henry Ford once pointed out, whether you think you *can* or think you *can't*, either way you'll be right. Success is all about attitude, and it is no different with money.

Most people have some kind of limiting beliefs when it comes to money. I was recently working with a freelance TV researcher, who was charging below market rates for her time. When I asked what was stopping her increasing her daily rate she said she felt she wasn't worth more. Think about your own beliefs about money. If you have spent the last five years in debt, does that mean you will always be up to your eyes in bill payments? NO! If you have always lived week to week, does that mean the next 20 years of your life will be the same? NO! However, the answer to these questions could easily be YES if you are not prepared to identify any issues you have with money, and learn to use money as a tool to improve your future.

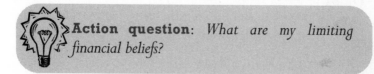

Action question: *What are my limiting financial beliefs?*

To move beyond your self-limiting financial beliefs, you need to believe that financial security and freedom are possible. As with any other goals, if you can't visualize or imagine these things, it is unlikely that you will look for opportunities to help you achieve financial freedom. From a sociological perspective, our early experiences of money are clearly the source of our attitudes as adults. When you were growing up, were you told, "Money doesn't grow on trees"? Or that "Money doesn't buy you happiness—or love"? Maybe you heard "Money is the root of all evil," or "We simply can't afford that." Change your beliefs about money. Replace those negative beliefs with positive, affirming beliefs about your financial freedom or security: "I am enjoying financial freedom," or "I am always financially secure."

Choose to put your old beliefs behind you. There are many respectable opportunities for achieving financial freedom. Being financially secure is something we can all aspire to in a healthy way. How different would your life and your relationship with money be if you believed it could be used to achieve your dreams? If it could be used to help you achieve work/life balance? Interestingly, I have yet to find a wealthy individual who doesn't appreciate the luxuries that money can buy. Remember, money won't make your life perfect, but it can certainly help you pursue your big dreams in life.

 Action task: Identify your limiting beliefs about money. Decide what new beliefs you would like to replace these with.

Find opportunities for generating passive income

Every book you will ever read about the secrets of the rich talks about passive income. Passive income is the ideal way to increase your income. Who wouldn't like to earn money while they sleep or while they are relaxing on a tropical island? It's a lovely idea, and with a bit of planning you can find opportunities for passive income. Passive income can come from investments, property (not the house you live in), royalties from books/music, or a business that doesn't require your daily involvement.

Many people set up their own businesses thinking it is the ultimate way to generate a healthy income. However, many small-business owners fall into the trap of billing their time, which means they are merely self-employed. This means that if you are ill, not working or reach your maximum billable hours, your income is limited. If you own your own business, standardize your operations so it is able to function in your absence and ultimately can be sold at some time in the future.

Additional resource: I highly recommend Michael E. Gerber's bestseller, *The E-Myth Revisited* (HarperBusiness, 1995), for more information on this strategy.

Think long term

Instant gratification is our biggest enemy when it comes to financial freedom. Would you like to go out to dinner every Friday night, or would you forgo this and other luxuries for financial freedom in 10 years' time? Most people, given a choice, will opt for the immediate pleasure. It is easy to see why so many people put off planning for retirement or their children's education. Thinking long term is easier when you have a strong vision and clear goals in life, but acting long term requires dedication and discipline. I regularly find flyers for get-rich-quick schemes in our mail box which certainly sound tempting, but most financial planners say it takes on average a decade to reach financial freedom.

Remember, if you are saving for a vacation, car or wedding, you are spending, not saving to invest for your financial future. Yes, it is important to live life, and I would never deny anyone the opportunity to enjoy themselves, but you should always have a long-term strategy in place.

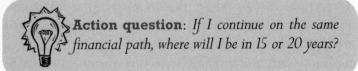

Action question: *If I continue on the same financial path, where will I be in 15 or 20 years?*

While we are talking long-term planning, the most distant goal most of us can imagine is our retirement. The big question of how much you will actually need when you retire depends on several factors, including the income you want to live on when you retire, and the age at which you plan to retire. You have little control over what the government will provide, so plan conservatively.

Now, as a reformed "I'm not good with numbers" girl, I would like to make a suggestion. If you think all this financial planning involves too much paperwork, or you don't understand what it all means, get expert advice or increase your knowledge so you can take control of your finances. Susanna Stuart believes the difference between financial struggle and success usually comes down to your degree of knowledge.

"Sometimes through not knowing, people are paralyzed into inaction and never improve their wealth," she explains.

You can increase your financial knowledge by reading books, using online tools, and attending seminars and courses. Aim to understand what your accountant, advisor or banker is saying so you can make informed choices.

Regardless of your degree of knowledge, you may wish to seek quality advice to ensure a long-term approach to your financial planning. If you are looking for a financial advisor, shop around, ask questions, and check that your advisor is qualified and that they are a member of the independent professional body CFA (Certified Financial Planner Board of Standards). Don't invest without a written plan from your advisor, and remember to review your plan at least annually.

Additional resource: Find a financial advisor through www.cfp.net

Take control of your finances

Rather than procrastinating over your finances a moment longer, take control, seek professional advice if necessary and determine your financial plan. Like any other goals, your finances require careful attention and specific actions. In Chapter 2, I will show you in detail how to organize your finances so you can move beyond living week to week, waiting for your paycheck to balance your checkbook.

The best thing you can do to take control of your finances is clarify where your money goes. What is your income, what are your expenses, what assets do you have, what are you really worth? Many people don't have a clear picture of their financial status, so here's a net worth equation everyone needs to complete:

Net worth = assets minus liabilities
            (what you own)   (what you owe)

As Susanna Stuart explains, your net worth is a snapshot of your financial position.

"Understanding what makes up your net worth is the first step—knowing what your assets and liabilities are. The second step is analyzing the assets—wealth-creating versus lifestyle—and also analyzing the debts. The third step is to then make the best use of the resources."

First, Susanna suggests you write down what you own and what you owe—the difference is your net worth. Although it is a simple idea, many people find it quite frightening. But if you have more assets (property, cars, investments) than liabilities (mortgage, loans, debts) you are in a good position. Having more liabilities than assets is not an ideal position, but at least having a realistic picture of your current financial situation means you can begin to plan accordingly. Take a closer look at how your investments are performing (if you have any) or if you are spending more than you earn.

Action task: Gain a clear snapshot of your own financial position by listing what you own, minus what you owe. Use this information as a starting point for financial planning.

Here are Susanna Stuart's top six tips to help you focus on your financial freedom:

- Keep debt under control and use it to invest in wealth-creating assets rather than consumption.

- Work out your personal financial plan and strategy. Remember, wealth-creation strategies need time to work, so don't leave it to the last minute.
- Have two to three months' salary set aside in a savings account as an emergency fund.
- Review your financial plan every one to two years. Changes in the economy, tax or your personal circumstances may mean you need to make changes to your plan.
- Any investment advice you receive should be tailored to your personal goals, risk profile, time-frame and tax status.
- Have a current will.

Get focused: chapter summary

Focus on your dreams
- Think big
- Find your passion
- Create your vision
- Turn the dream into reality
- Prioritize your goals

Focus on your priorities
- Discover your purpose
- Live your values
- Find work you love

Focus on people
- Build a strong network of family and friends
- Look to role models

- Use a mentor
- Start coaching
- Create your own *Stop Living Your Job, Start Living Your Life* motivational group
- Network formally

Focus on financial freedom

- Pursue your dreams
- Set financial goals and make a plan
- Change your beliefs about money
- Find opportunities for generating passive income
- Think long term
- Take control of your finances.

Chapter 2

Get organized

Before everything else, getting ready is the secret of success.
— HENRY FORD

You are answering urgent emails, simultaneously sorting correspondence, the phone is ringing, you are running five minutes late for a meeting, you have to finish a project before 4 p.m., and you have said yes to a farewell party and then a dinner when you finish work, although you already know you will be late for both. When you finally get home you know you will be up for several more hours preparing for an 8 a.m. meeting the next day, as you simply haven't had time to look at the material before now. Meanwhile your home looks like a bomb site, with dirty laundry piling up and household chores left undone. Does this sound like a version of your life?

In the search for balance you just need to get organized to create time and space in your life for your personal priorities. By organizing and effectively planning your daily life you will be able to focus on your big picture and vision for life.

Having efficient systems in place to help you find what you need quickly works well both at home and at work.

You might balk at the time needed to organize information, but ultimately it is a fraction of the time you would waste searching for information you can't find.

 Quick quiz: How organized are you?

- Do you feel rushed trying to get ready for the day?
- Do you often have to search for your wallet, keys or cell phone?
- Do you constantly feel you are running out of time?
- Do you have piles of mail that need to be opened?
- Do you write notes on bits of scratch paper?
- Do you waste time trying to locate files?
- Do you often have to cancel appointments because of unexpected demands on your time?
- Do you have to search for your bank statements?
- Do you frequently miss payment deadlines because you can't find the bills?
- Is it typical to be hounded for expired car registrations and insurance policies?
- Do you write "to do" lists but never seem to check the "done" box?
- Do you feel you never have your "head above water"?
- Do you keep trying to find time to exercise but never do?
- Do you often get to the gym and realize you don't have all your gear?
- Do you keep planning to do "important things" like writing a will or retirement planning but never do?

Score: Did you get a perfect score and answer "No" to every question? It is more likely that you answered "Yes" to quite a few questions, highlighting how your organization and time-management skills can be developed to simplify your life. Depending on your score, you may choose to adopt some of the following strategies for time and daily-life management. In Chapter 1 you identified your personal priorities; now you can use the concepts, tools and techniques detailed here to help you align your priorities so you have time to work on balancing your life.

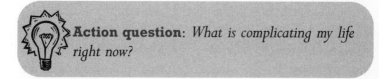 **Action question**: *What is complicating my life right now?*

Organize your time

If you are constantly amazed at people who live a calmer life than you do, take charge of the time you have. If you are busy all the time you may think you are being efficient, but the reality is often the opposite. In my research, 39% of survey respondents said that time management was their biggest work/life balance challenge. The reality is that we all have exactly 24 hours every day. Consider for a moment: if you did have an extra hour a day, how would you spend it? Perhaps you would use the time for yourself. Nearly all our clients say they are striving for more "me time." In fact, time to exercise or socialize is often the first thing to be dropped off our schedules when we are busy. Working long hours isn't necessarily a problem if you don't feel you are neglecting other areas of your life. However, if you are feeling frustrated because you don't seem to be able to find time to prepare healthy food, exercise or relax, then you need to give yourself a reality check. How are you really spending your time? Working smarter, not harder, is the aim of time management; ultimately you want to be able to choose to spend your time on tasks that produce the greatest satisfaction or add value to your life-balance goals. Use the following strategies to reclaim your time.

Minimize time-traps

Minimizing time-guzzlers can be as simple as screening phone calls. Sounds simple, doesn't it? And it can be, if you identify where your time is being wasted and eliminate the problem at the source. Classic time-traps include telephone calls, checking your emails as they arrive, endless meetings, interruptions, web surfing, not being able to say "No" assertively, not prioritizing tasks or a non-existent schedule. Be honest about the amount of your time that is being wasted, and include time at home, where a classic time-trap is television.

Action task: List your top 10 personal time-traps. Don't get depressed about how much time is being wasted, but consciously address each time-guzzler. What can you do to overcome each time-trap?

I used to channel-surf all night, but now I check out the TV listings and only watch what I really want to watch. It means I now have more time for friends, family and interests.

— JANET, 53, DESIGNER

Track your time

In *Aspirations*, I introduced the "Seven-Day Time Tracker." This concept involves logging your time so you can increase your awareness of where and how you actually spend it. By analyzing this information you can learn a lot about the patterns of daily interruptions and how to break them.

Tracking your time is also important since old-fashioned prescriptive time-management plans often overlook your individual reality. It is impossible to make sustainable changes without knowledge of your current situation. Take up the challenge to review how you spend your time over the next week and highlight any additional time-traps that you may not have identified in the previous strategy.

Action task: Review your time log and either high-light or underline what is absolutely essential for maintaining the life you want to lead. Then look at the remaining items and ask yourself whether it is possible not to do the task, to delegate it (see delegation strategy later in this chapter) or at least to do it less often.

Plan a realistic schedule

Plan your day ahead of time, using a weekly and monthly overview, plus a daily focus. Don't wait for the day to begin and then panic when you become aware of the 101 things that must be done. Block out time for specific commitments so you can focus on your priorities and become truly effective. Set aside large blocks of time or designate time zones for specific kinds of activities. For example, time zones at work might include administration, business development, meetings and clients. At home you might regularly block out time for study, sport, recreation, hobbies, home projects and of course chores and household management.

Whether you use an electronic diary, a computer or a paper-based scheduling system is your choice. This will depend on your lifestyle and preferences. Each system has its pros and cons, so choose what will work best for you and then stick with it. Whatever you choose, use only one diary, planner or organizer, to avoid double-booking yourself. That said, I often encourage clients to represent their year visually on a large wall planner which can give an instant overview and focus for the months to come.

The easiest way to plan a realistic schedule is to set sensible deadlines, prioritize your "to do" list within your schedule and group tasks together. In effect, what you are doing is reallocating your time to the things that are most important in your life, which you identified in Chapter 1. Grouping tasks together—like running errands, filing and paperwork—also increases your efficiency. Prioritize your "to do" list within your schedule, and keep each day's list short and realistic—restrict it to the top two or three things you must do that day. Having a list of 24 "must do's" in a day will just add to your anxiety and stress. Be brutal when planning your schedule—don't include items that you don't want to do, unless they serve a greater purpose in your long-term goals.

> **Hot tip:** *When you are up against the clock, ask yourself, "Is this the best use of my time, or is there a more efficient way to do this task?"*

Allow yourself planning time, and constantly review your schedule. Half an hour a day will probably be ample for most people, and using this time will ensure you are clear and focused throughout the day. Also, spend time preparing for forthcoming commitments. For example, if you are to speak at a conference in two months' time, when do you want to prepare your speech and begin practicing so you can deliver it with confidence? Plan in advance, factor it into your current schedule, and you will reduce your anxiety. I learned this technique when I worked in the media, where we used to refer constantly to our "forward planner" at weekly team meetings. While we still had to focus on the current week's work, planning ahead in our diaries for the next few months gave us a better focus on stories and campaigns that we could expect in the near future.

Action task: Use your computer scheduler or draw up a table on a piece of paper, dividing your day into reasonable time blocks. Think back to when you had a schedule at school. What you are doing here is providing a framework for your time. Some common themes I use for timetabling include afternoons for client meetings, time for project work and regular daily time periods for administration. Outside of work, consider your routine of reading the weekend newspapers, socializing, designating "homework" time for your children and family visits.

I like to keep my schedule simple and I always give myself more time than I think I might need, as things can sometimes take a lot longer than you anticipate.

— MELANIE, 30, HR MANAGER

Manage phone use

We have already identified phone calls as a potential time-trap. Unless you work in a call center, phone calls can seriously interrupt your flow of work, not to mention your concentration. Manage your phone time more effectively by coming to grips with the technology—learn to use speed dial and other special features on your phone. When there is a backlog on your answering machine or voice mail, write down messages then delete them immediately. That way you won't have to scroll through old messages next time you check them. As a coach, I find a headset is vital as it frees my hands to take notes and enables me to refer to paperwork while on a call. It also has ergonomic benefits by reducing the "phone to ear, crick in neck" syndrome. If you spend a lot of time on the phone, consider using a hands-free headset. Using a mobile hands-free set is an important safety consideration when you are driving too.

It may sound like telephone etiquette, but when you have someone in your office, don't take a call, and don't answer your cell phone when you are with someone—this distracts everyone and wastes time by diffusing your concentration. When blocking out time for similar tasks it makes sense to make all your phone calls together. It is much faster to make 10 consecutive calls than to spread them throughout the day, and it will definitely help you keep your calls short and effective. Just as you would prepare for an appointment by gathering together any relevant paperwork, do the same when it comes to phone calls—have all the necessary information at hand.

I am sometimes accused of being antisocial when I screen phone calls with an answering machine or caller ID. However, the phone is my biggest time-trap. By answering every call I am in effect making the call a priority, when in reality I may have more pressing priorities. I am not suggesting you should ignore your phone for days on end, but be smart about how you take and make calls. For example, use voice mail for an hour so you can create solid blocks of uninterrupted time. Then you are able to cluster your return calls together. If you are uncomfortable with this, you might choose to answer only your cell and to screen your landline, assuming most people will try your cell if they need to get in touch with you urgently. The idea behind ignoring your phone to create uninterrupted time is that nothing is really so important that it can't wait. While there are always exceptions, more often than not it is the caller who hasn't planned their time efficiently and is passing on their stress to you as they rush to meet what they perceive as a last-minute deadline.

Hot tip: *When you are leaving a voice-mail message remember to include detailed information to minimize call-backs. Give a specific time when you can be called back or when you will try to return a call. Better still, break out of the phone-tag cycle and send an email!*

Set boundaries for quiet time

In the previous strategy I suggested switching off your phone for an hour to provide a block of uninterrupted time. Imagine having an hour or two free of distractions so you are able to concentrate on important project work. I have seen many stressed-out executives who, as an absolute last resort, close their door and say, "No interruptions." Why not be proactive and let your team or colleagues know why you need quiet time and how you can achieve it together? In some corporate organizations I have worked with, teams collectively set regular daily quiet times, while in other organizations individuals might put a sign on their door or workstation to communicate that they are concentrating and do not want to be disturbed. Certainly, setting boundaries for quiet time does require assertive communication. This can often be the first barrier people face in setting the system in place. Once you have established the boundary, make sure everyone knows you are serious about your new work habit by committing to the "do not disturb" time slots you have diligently told everyone about. When you are planning your realistic schedule perhaps you might also choose to set aside solid, regular blocks of uninterrupted time. Designating "quiet times" can work wonders at home, too.

Tune into your body clock

We all know whether we are a morning person or a night owl. Choose to work the hours that suit you best and exercise when your energy is at a peak. It is often a good idea to get your hardest work done during your peak hours, too. Don't worry about your colleagues or friends—focus on your own body clock. If you are not sleeping well, exercising or eating well-balanced, frequent meals you may have unhealthy energy peaks and valleys. If you are constantly tired, seek professional help to rule out any medical conditions that may be impacting on your life.

Trade time

Before you take on a new commitment, either at work or at home, eliminate something that you don't need or want to do any more. This sounds like an easy strategy and it is. So often we take on a new commitment to prove that we can do it, or because we feel we are expected to. In Chapter 1, I asked you to take a closer look at your values and priorities—so revisit them if you are struggling to trade time. Ask yourself, if you didn't have to live with the consequences of saying "No," would you have agreed to that extra work project, volunteer work or invitation?

 Action question: *Does this new activity or commitment honor my values and will it help me achieve my vision of an ideal life?*

Organize your daily life

While managing your time is an excellent tool, organizing your daily life means taking a closer look at the systems you can use to create ongoing efficiency. Organizing your life will free up your thoughts to focus on your vision of an ideal life.

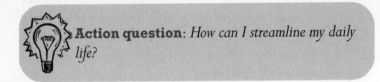

Action question: *How can I streamline my daily life?*

Use technology to your advantage

Increasingly, the boundaries between work and life are being blurred by technology. While we were promised that technology would simplify our lives, the truth is that it also increases the amount of information in our lives and our output. Learn to use technology to your advantage, whether it is the Internet, managing your computer files or your emails.

Internet

The great thing about the Internet is that you can use it to literally find any fact in seconds. Test it out yourself by finding a phone number online, rather than referring to your hard-copy directory. There are also free-to-use dictionaries, currency converters and a favorite site of mine, www.timeanddate.com, which you can use to determine time differences across the globe.

A time-saver I have been using recently is my local library's online catalog. From my office I can peruse the catalog, so when I arrive at the library I can skip the line to use their computers and go straight to the book I want. Better still, if the book isn't available I can reserve it online and be notified via email when it arrives—all without leaving home, battling traffic, finding a parking space and wasting time.

Aside from online directories, the Internet is a

fabulous way to research quickly, but remember to be discerning in your selections, especially if you are looking for "official" information. The Internet also has the advantage of being updated frequently, meaning you are accessing the latest news and information.

You can use search engines such as www.google.com to find virtually anything you could ever need. Choose a search engine you can understand and use it to streamline your queries. Simplify your Internet use even further by saving the sites you frequently access as "Favorites." You might also want to use the Internet for banking, and to make advance or last-minute bookings at reduced rates for travel and entertainment.

Email

First, tell your friends you don't want to be on their joke lists any more; this small tip can save you plenty of time and effort, and free you from constant distraction. Explain your reason for not wanting to receive your colleagues' or friends' jokes. The reality is, if we read every joke we received, our entire day could be taken up with "funnies."

Deal with emails like paper—once you have read a message, file it, schedule a time to deal with it, or delete it so it doesn't linger in your inbox where you might read it several times. When it comes to organizing your incoming emails, treat your inbox like a physical desktop: keep it clear except for the items you are working on. Whether you work from home or in an office, learn how you can "sort" incoming emails on your system. Microsoft Outlook, for example, has an "organize" feature, sorting emails into appropriate folders immediately without any effort on your part. This means you can look at relevant messages in the time you have designated for their attention, rather than spending additional time sorting a bulging inbox. This is a great way to keep personal emails separate from work-related items too.

Use the preview feature on your email program. This will show you the first few lines of the message, meaning that if it's junk mail or a virus you can delete it without wasting any further time.

How often do you reply "Thanks" to an email when you really don't need to? Similarly, if you don't require a reply, tell the recipient, "No reply needed." This is another simple tip that saves everyone time and reduces the number of emails cluttering your inbox unnecessarily.

When replying to messages, keep the original subject headings, as this makes it easier to track a discussion, especially if you are waiting for a reply before you act on a task. Save time while you promote your business by setting up an electronic signature that lists all your contact details.

Resist the temptation to be online continuously by designating times to read and act on your emails, just as you would read regular correspondence. Set specific times during the day to check your email so you don't constantly interrupt your work. I have clients who check messages at the beginning of the day, at lunchtime and at the end of the day. Evaluate your work situation and decide what is appropriate for you. You may be able to allocate one time block a day to deal with emails, or if your role requires a higher level of online attention you may choose to check every two hours. If you find the habit of constantly checking messages hard to break, start by turning off the "You have new mail" pop-up window, since it will only encourage you to check your emails as they arrive.

Computer

Keep your computer desktop clear of clutter and only display program icons you use regularly. Just as you would organize a traditional filing cabinet, do the same with files on your computer. Use a logical process in naming documents and filing them. Keep different projects in separate folders that are clearly identifiable. Including a date in a filename allows you to identify the most up-to-date version of a document.

Make use of document templates; not only are they excellent for saving time, they also provide a high level of consistency and professionalism in your communications. This is vital for executives, who are increasingly relied upon to manage their own administration rather than using support staff.

Back up your hard drive! *Sex & the City*'s Carrie famously learned the dangers of not backing up when everything she had ever written was lost after her laptop crashed. Make the back-up process part of your planning or administration basics.

Manage paper flow

The idea of a paperless office is largely a myth. Even in our office, where the majority of communication is via email or the telephone, we still receive a huge amount of paper from outside sources and this information needs to be screened efficiently. There is also no denying that you do need hard copies of certain documents for legal purposes. Create a system of reference or archive files for this important information. In addition, have a system for general working files that you have easy access to. There are hundreds of ideas on how to manage paper-based filing systems, including basic color coding, alphabetical order and more complex ideas, so test your method for accessibility and if necessary investigate more efficient options.

Action task: To test if your filing system is working for you, set aside five minutes to find the following information: last year's tax return, a bank statement from January 2003 and your life insurance policy.

This action task illustrates that whatever system you use, the true test is whether you are able to locate the information you need instantly. Think logically about where you file your records and then you will be able to locate them in a few seconds.

Before you even contemplate filing material, learn to manage the flow of information. A simple system of paper trays for incoming and outgoing correspondence, and a "pending" file, can work for many people. Beware of dumping everything into the "pending" file though! Create a simple filing system for all your loose papers. Daily file categories could be sorted into action areas such as call, order, pay, read, discuss, etc. A system that works well for me is hanging files labeled "Monday" to "Friday" for upcoming meeting and client notes. I've also seen a numerical file numbered 1–31 for days of the month. Remember, the key to any filing system is the index. Systems can fail because the same information can be stored under a number of different categories. You can use a simple spreadsheet or a more sophisticated software program to generate an index.

Avoid collecting scraps of paper with messages and notes on them. As a journalist I learned always to have a spiral notebook with me for unexpected interviews or to jot down ideas. As I progressed through my media career I kept using notebooks so I always had a record of my messages and notes in the one place. Having one notebook in your central work area is practical; however, I have developed this idea and always have a notebook with me, either in a handbag, car glove compartment, gym bag or on the bedside table! This way, no matter where I am or what I am doing, a piece of paper on which to jot down information is never far away. Store your used notebooks in a drawer for six months in case there is any information you need to refer to, then throw them out.

Be strict about handling each piece of paper only once, especially if you can spend less than two minutes dealing with it. If you are sorting through information, correspondence or messages, try to act on them immediately. If something will require more than half an hour of your time, schedule an appropriate time to deal with it— don't just put it in a "to do" file.

A conference participant shared with me recently a very easy and useful concept called the 4D's:

- Do it now
- Deal with it later (but schedule time for this)
- Delegate it
- Ditch, dump or delete it.

Action question: *Next time you pick up a piece of paper in your home or work environment, ask yourself, "Can I—Do it now? Schedule a time to Deal with it later? Delegate it? or Ditch it?"*

If you haven't got storage facilities you will never really control your paperwork. Remember the space closest to you is the most precious, especially if you have a desk or workstation. Use drawers at arm's length for items you need often, such as paper, envelopes or stapler.

Storing material upright rather than flat in a pile is another common-sense idea that will simplify your approach to paperwork. Remember, "File, don't pile." I saw an example of this recently with a client who, despite a messy desk and piles of papers, was certain he could locate anything he needed. Yet when I asked him to find the notes from our last session he was soon stumped, and moving around pile upon pile of paperwork.

Many people mistakenly think they don't need to be organized at home as it's not a business environment. Perhaps if you are already organized at work you could transfer a few ideas into managing your household, too. We all have bills to pay, bank statements arriving, school notices, invitations, magazine subscriptions and other information that can be effectively dealt with, delegated, done or deleted!

I have five people to support at work in an administrative capacity. I use a special "blue book" where I record who asked for what, when they asked for it, what it is and when they need it by. Then I go through my book several times a day and once I have completed something, I cross it off. A little tick next to an item is just not gratifying enough for me, I need to cross it off completely.

— ANNALIESE, 26

SALES AND MARKETING ASSISTANT

Prepare ahead of time

Set your week in motion by identifying what you want to accomplish. Earlier I discussed using a diary to plan your time and help you with this.

I use the Girl Scouts' motto "Be prepared" to keep me on track. Being prepared is one of the easiest things you can do to help create a better work/life balance. If I prepare for a meeting, event or project I can lighten my stress load, knowing that I have everything under control to the best of my ability. A key area that clients often ask for coaching on is preparing ahead of time for meetings. Often, meetings use agendas to keep people on track—but don't use an agenda for the sake of it, use it to focus your team and lift your performance as a group. Circulate background information before a meeting so you can launch into a discussion rather than spending unnecessary time getting everyone up to speed. That way you, and everyone else, can also do your homework before the meeting, then contribute or ask intelligent questions that will ultimately move you all forward as a team. Block out a specific time beforehand for doing this—preparation isn't flicking through a discussion document in your 30-second elevator ride.

> *I plan for the next day before I go to bed. I get up early so I can have a head start on the day before the family gets up.*
>
> — LYNN, 46, TEACHER'S AIDE

Delegate

Before you ignore this strategy let me explain that delegation isn't just for managers in the workplace. Delegation is a skill we can all use in many areas of our lives, including at home. The idea behind successful delegation is that taking charge of your life doesn't mean doing absolutely everything yourself. Delegate what you feel most comfortable handing over to someone else, and make use of people's specialist skills.

When you are overwhelmed with things to do, it can feel like you don't have the time to utilize delegation as a strategy. Don't fall into the "I'm too busy to delegate" or "It's quicker to do it myself" trap. Setting aside a small amount of time to decide what and how you can delegate will provide you with more time in the long run.

Don't feel guilty dumping work on others, since that's not what you are doing. It is most likely that the task you are delegating is something you don't enjoy doing, or you realize your time could be better used elsewhere. We all have different skills, and delegation works best when you match the right person to the job. Seriously consider delegating jobs you aren't good at or simply don't enjoy. Also consider repetitive tasks such as gardening, grocery shopping, book-keeping and housework, and then look at special projects such as decorating, planning a vacation, or buying a new car or computer.

Delegation is a three-stage process that involves presenting the task, being available for guidance while the job is being done and then evaluating the outcome. When you delegate a task, people need to know they are making a valuable contribution and are part of a team. Even if you are paying someone to help, a "Thank you" is a powerful acknowledgement.

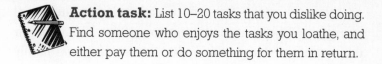 **Action task:** List 10–20 tasks that you dislike doing. Find someone who enjoys the tasks you loathe, and either pay them or do something for them in return.

Schedule for spontaneity and interruptions

Avoid planning your day in such minute detail that you can't cope with unexpected demands that then turn into high priorities. In our first coaching session, Duncan (49) identified a need to seriously rearrange his schedule to cope with demands in his senior management role. He was extremely frustrated at the "firefighting" or unexpected interruptions he was expected to deal with and manage on a daily basis. Instead of planning enough work for a solid eight-hour day, he chose to plan for a five-hour workload, which left three hours to deal with staff demands and unexpected items.

In short, plan on being interrupted—if it's inevitable that your day will have constant interruptions it is vital to allow room for them in your schedule rather than becoming sidetracked by them. Like Duncan, don't necessarily expect to do a solid eight hours' work in an eight-hour day. Instead, schedule six hours for work (or whatever is realistic in your work situation) and block off two hours for interruptions or, rather, spontaneity.

Make it a date!

This is a strategy numerous clients have adopted to provide non-negotiable time for events that are important in their lives. It might be time specifically for exercising, for your partner or family, or for "me time."

Recently Susan (34), who was working toward a goal of creating a home environment to nurture her children's development, designated Wednesday evenings as "family night." This simple idea ensured all the family were together to enjoy a meal and relax in each other's company. A regular family night can be especially effective for families whose working week seems to be entirely consumed by after-school activities and events.

If you find it hard to catch up with friends, use the same idea and "make it a date" for a regular Sunday brunch or night out once a month. This means you can all commit to a fun time, and can plan in advance for things like childcare. You also don't have to waste time trying to match gaps in your schedules in order to see each other.

Finding time for ourselves as individuals, however, appears to be the most challenging. You keep appointments with other people, so how about making appointments with yourself for the things that really matter? Do you often start the week with great intentions of exercising then simply run out of time? Factor in fitness by scheduling in your gym classes, use a personal trainer who you are committed to or join a sports team so you will stick to your appointment.

Dedicate time for yourself in which you can relax, unwind and rejuvenate. Running your life at 100 miles per hour is not sustainable in the long term, as you will learn in Chapter 3.

Action task: The 10-minute challenge—spend 10 minutes every day simply doing nothing! Make this part of your regular self-care, as a way of switching off, de-stressing and relaxing. You might choose to meditate, breathe or do gentle stretches.

When I've made time to go to the gym, I also schedule 45 minutes while the kids are still in child care so I can relax in the café and read a book for myself, as this is the only time out I have in a week.

— MARY, 38, STUDENT AND MOTHER

Be smart and multitask

We have all heard the saying "To kill two birds with one stone," which means to accomplish two separate tasks in a single effort. It's smart to multitask. Consider cycling or walking to work to double up on your commuting and exercise efforts. Why not try exercising with friends so you can socialize and get fit at the same time? Make two meals at once and freeze one—this saves time, effort and power. Make use of traveling and waiting time by returning quick phone calls or catching up on reading.

Action task: Revisit your time log, review your newly formed schedule and identify areas where you can creatively multitask. Maybe it's doing your banking when you are at the supermarket? Writing birthday cards or letters while at the hairdresser's? Having breakfast/lunch meetings for work? List 10 ways you can simplify your life through multitasking.

Organize your space

If you want to make real changes in your life, you need to have enough space to do so. This clarity often comes by giving our lives a spring cleaning. Now is the perfect time to spring-clean your life by removing physical clutter and creating the vital space you need to focus on your personal priorities. Clearing clutter will have an immediate impact on your life by giving you more time to focus on your bigger picture. From a practical point of view, clearing clutter and reorganizing your daily life will mean you can instantly find your keys, locate important files and take control of the small stuff.

> **Action question**: *Every time you sit down today, either at work or at home, look around and ask yourself, "Do I really need this item?" This is an easy first step for clearing clutter.*

Clear clutter

Start the process by making your own list of 10 or more things that you are putting up with. What are you tolerating in your life? Is it an untidy office, unreturned phone calls, a bulging email inbox, a messy wardrobe in dire need of maintenance, an overdue oil change for your car, a cluttered pantry or spare room, or unorganized bills and personal papers? Consider reorganizing cupboards, filing cabinets and drawers. Evaluate your home and work environments and identify the areas that need your attention. What items can you do without? What needs to be replaced? What could be better used elsewhere?

Select two items from your list and take action to eliminate them by the end of the week. Gradually work at eliminating everything on your list. This process may be ongoing, but make a commitment to being aware of what is cluttering your life and ultimately holding you back from living your best life. Before you begin, you might like to spend a few minutes imagining how much more streamlined and simple your life is going to be when your home or work environment is clutter free.

If you are not sure where to start, relax, because it really doesn't matter. The important thing is that you start *somewhere*—as soon as you do this you are more than halfway there. Remember, procrastination (see Chapter 5) often creates more stress and anxiety than just doing what you need to do. Be strong, and don't let yourself be overwhelmed at the idea of clearing clutter. Take a deep breath and focus on one small area. Once that area is done you will build up momentum, and before long you will be in a clutter-free zone. If you are more spontaneous, challenge yourself to a weekly 10-minute clear-out. Walk through your home or workplace and find 10 items that you want to discard or give away.

Clutter-clearing tips:

- **What's bothering you the most?** This is usually the best place to begin. If you hate that pile of papers on your desk, start there. If your frustration is rising because you can't fit another item on the kitchen table, then start there.
- **Focus on a little bit at a time.** Rather than thinking about the huge job ahead, break the project into smaller, more manageable tasks. For instance, if you want to organize the boxes in your spare room, consider going through one box a day until the job is completed. Or if your filing cabinet needs the once-over, attack each

drawer separately rather than fighting a paper war.

- **Reward yourself.** While not everyone will find the task of clearing clutter enjoyable, the end result is certainly refreshing. If you need added motivation to get going, choose a personal incentive. You might promise yourself half an hour reading a new novel or having a coffee with a friend if you clear a specific area of clutter. A small reward will certainly ensure you get your task finished promptly.
- **Use support.** Buddy up with a friend, neighbor or coach and commit to dates and times to deal with your clutter. By doing this you will have added accountability.
- **Boost your spirits.** The ultimate way to have fun while clearing clutter is to listen to your favorite CD—definitely a way to stay alert, and it can make the more tedious tasks pass a little faster.

Not ready?

Sometimes it can be difficult to part with items that have been important to you at some point in time. Here's a trick you can use to make sure you have no regrets. Box up anything you are not ready to let go of and make a note to review it in the future. If you haven't used anything from the box in six months' time, you may feel more comfortable letting go.

What next?

Cleaning out your clutter can be very freeing. You will find yourself boxing up items you haven't used in 10 years, finding old treasures you had forgotten about, and making room for items that you use all the time. Throughout your spring-cleaning sessions, if an item is of absolutely no use to anyone, be ruthless and throw it out. Consider selling items, donating to charity and recycling. Maybe hold a garage sale with friends or neighbors who have also spring-cleaned their homes and lives.

Set yourself some ground rules when clearing clutter so you are propelled into taking action. Here are some ideas to get you started.

Kitchen:

- Discard anything past its use-by date in the fridge or pantry.
- Put all your loose-leaf recipes into one folder or scrapbook.
- Use a grocery list or copy a standard list and tick off your weekly requirements.

Bathroom:

- Discard old medication, especially those that are past their expiration date or not clearly identified.
- Recycle half-used bottles of shampoo and body products.

Wardrobe:

- Discard anything that doesn't fit properly, hasn't been worn in the last year, doesn't make you feel great or you simply don't like.
- Don't put away items that need maintenance: fix them.
- Group similar items of clothing together so you can find what you need at a moment's notice. Choose to sort by color, dress code or garment type.

Paperwork:

- Discard anything that is out of date, such as school notices, meeting agendas, invitations for events that have already passed and brochures for products you have already bought.
- Magazines and newspapers piling up? Sort them out! Will you really read last week's Sunday paper? Unless you are absolutely dying to read it—recycle it.

Office:

- Only have current work on your desktop so you have room to move.
- Clear your desk drawers and keep items you use daily close to hand.
- Make it a regular habit to put work away at the end of the day.

Car:

- Use a rubbish bag and empty it regularly; this will make an instant difference to a cluttered car.
- If you like to keep some sports/outdoor gear in your trunk, perhaps use large plastic boxes to keep things tidy.
- Think of your security and clear out your valuables, or don't keep them in your car at all.
- Don't forget to have maps, first-aid kits, repair equipment and emergency service numbers in the car so you are prepared for any eventuality.

Put systems in place

Once you have cleared the clutter, put in place maintenance systems to ensure you don't fall back into old habits. Don't try complicated ideas; stick to processes that are easy, work for you and fit your lifestyle. Keep in mind that the new processes you put in place are to make you more efficient. While a color-coded, cross-referenced filing system may look like a good idea—will you really use it?

Action task: Each week for the next few months choose to clear clutter in one particular area—desk, filing cabinet, cupboards, car, kitchen, etc. When you have cleared the clutter, ask yourself how you would like to use the space and put in place systems that support your idea.

Have a home for everything

Professional organizers say the most important thing you can do once you have cleared clutter is to find a home for everything. This is done most easily by zoning your space at home and work for the most efficient use.

Catherine Smith is a leading personal organizer. She uses the analogy of a kindergarten:

> *The blocks, dress-up hats, paintbrushes and books are not jumbled into big piles, but zoned into logical groups. There's a reading corner with books and pillows, and then there's the art corner, blocks corner and other specific play areas.*

She recommends zoning your home and work environments in the same way, with areas for particular activities. "Being organized does not mean we have to be clutter-free minimalists," she says.

Catherine is passionate about creating environments that inspire people to make space in their lives for the things that matter.

"The point is to have things we need every day easily at hand," she says, adding that being organized has helped her find balance in life and live more simply.

Catherine's top space-organizing tips:

- Start by tossing the easy stuff! This gives you a sense of achievement and gets you into a ruthless "Do I need this any more?" groove.
- For immediate impact, move the big items first. You'll feel an instant lift by shifting something like a piece of furniture or a big box.
- Remind yourself why you are clearing clutter. You are not de-cluttering to win the Home of the Year award. You want to find that CD easily, put your hands on bills to pay before they become overdue, or relax in your bedroom without a pile of ironing collapsing on you.
- Clear then replace; empty absolutely everything out of a drawer or off the surface that you are reorganizing. Sort it and only put back what you want to keep. This is much easier than shifting piles of clutter from one place to another.
- Don't try to reorganize your home or office in one day. Think "little and often." Limit your clearing sessions to 30 minutes or an hour so you avoid procrastinating. Organize your DVDs one time, the magazine pile the next, the junk pile by the telephone another time, and so on.

Organize your finances

Would you rather not think about your money situation? I find most clients don't want to know the truth about their financial situation as it means they will need to address it. The great thing about money management is that it is very tangible; you can use bank statements, receipts and budgets to track and measure your progress. In Chapter 1 we explored the "big-picture" vision for your life and the part that financial freedom or security plays in this. Here we take a closer look at how you can organize your finances on a day-to-day basis so that you spend less time worrying about whether or not you have the funds available to pay your rent or phone bill. This in turn will make you feel more in control of your life, helping you plan for a work/life balance. While some people see organizing finances as particularly tedious, especially if they like to be spontaneous or are creative souls, it will help you build your wealth so you are able to live the life you want in the future. Use these strategies to make the adjustments you need.

Establish your reality

Just like clearing clutter and managing your time, when organizing your money you need to start by being honest with yourself. In Chapter 1 we looked at how you can start taking control of your finances by discovering your net worth. This process is meaningless unless you give yourself a reality check on where the income you have is actually going, and areas you might like to change. Let's get back to basics and start by listing all your monthly expenses. I find that few people have any idea what they are actually spending their money on each month until they sit down and itemize every single expense. Yes, that includes newspapers, chocolate bars, lunches and gifts. This will give you a realistic idea of where you are right now and what you can do to organize your finances more efficiently. No excuses for lost receipts—obtain copies of your bank and credit card statements for the past few months and list all your expenditures.

When I asked a client recently what her monthly living expenses were, she couldn't tell me her baseline— that is, how much she needed to live her current life. Surprisingly, she was massively in debt, despite having an annual income of over $100,000. Because she was earning a high income she hadn't bothered to budget or plan ahead, thinking she could do everything on her pay. Like many of us, she had progressively lifted her living standards with every promotion or pay raise, assuming she could "afford" it all.

Action task: Write down exactly how you have spent your money over the last month; every bit of cash must be accounted for to give yourself a reality check on where your money goes.

Be brave and budget

It's not boring to budget—it's what successful people do to keep themselves on track. Remember, the first step in controlling your finances is knowing exactly where your money is going.

A budget is a plan of income and expenditure. It will tell you where you are now, and it will help you get to where you want to be. Your budget doesn't have to be rigid or restrictive and it can allow for impulsive spending. Setting and using a budget will encourage you to make conscious choices regarding your finances.

Like any goal, be realistic when setting your monthly budget. If you earn $3000 a month, it's unlikely that you will be able to save three-quarters of your income. It may seem like stating the obvious, but if your expenditure exceeds your income, find ways to minimize your expenses and increase your income.

Set your budget to suit your pay period and review it after every paycheck. Evaluate your progress by comparing your actual expenses with your budget. Here are standard budget areas you might incorporate:

- Rent/mortgage
- Savings/investments
- Loan repayments
- Insurances (health, life, car, homeowner's, etc.)
- Groceries (separate supermarket from other food such as lunches)
- Power (gas, electricity)
- Telephone (cell, landline)
- Car or commuting expenses (gas, maintenance)
- Big-ticket items (furniture, home renovation)
- Medical (include dental checkups, optometrists, etc.)
- Fitness (memberships, equipment)
- Clothing (include repairs, drycleaning)
- Grooming (include beauty products, haircuts)

- Entertainment (include dining, movies, music, etc.)
- Travel/vacations (flights, accommodation, campsites)
- Gifts for family and friends.

Also consider what point you are at in your life cycle—for example, are you saving for imminent retirement, your children's education or an overseas vacation? If so, budget for it. Don't forget to budget for incidentals such as magazines, drycleaning, subscriptions and presents—these "small" items can add up to thousands of dollars in a year. If you looked at them rationally you might choose to spend the money elsewhere, such as on an investment or a vacation.

Cut luxuries to save

A recent media report suggested that buying one less coffee a day over the course of a typical working life could mean a saving of $114,000. Savings like this can mean the difference between a comfortable future and a daily struggle. However, cutting luxuries is not a primary savings method—it's a way of trimming your expenses.

Action task: Revisit your budget and decide which "luxuries" you are prepared to forgo for the sake of your financial future. Make small adjustments and changes in your financial decisions now so you can set yourself up for the future. Consider cutting back on your luxury consumption rather than eliminating.

Automate

The biggest improvements to our banking system in recent years have been the introduction of phone and Internet banking. If you are a visual person you might prefer to "see" your bank balance online rather than listen to it on the phone. Whichever option you choose should offer you the benefits of being able to automate. Admittedly technology is moving at a fast rate, but be brave and keep up with the advances. If you have always used phone banking, find an hour to look at the options available to you online. Then decide which option is best for you.

Make life easy for yourself by paying your regular bills such as power, telephones and rent/mortgage by automatic payment. When you reconcile your accounts and check against your budget you will be able to ensure the correct payments have been processed.

Find out from your bank what their current transaction fees are and see if you can operate your account more efficiently. If you are disciplined you might decide to reduce your fees and simultaneously earn airline miles by paying all your bills automatically via your credit card. Pay off your credit card every month and you will reduce individual transaction fees.

Reduce debt

We all experience debt at varying stages of our lives, but when you decide to get smart about your money management, seek advice on how you can best reduce your debt. Choose to get out of debt and improve your financial position immediately. Why pay nearly 20% on credit card debt when your savings are only earning 5%? While there are two schools of thought on debt reduction and savings, based purely on numbers it makes sense to use any savings you have to pay off debt. Then you can start saving for your future.

If you have debts mounting from numerous credit cards, installment purchases, outstanding rent and overdue payments, consolidate your debt at a lower interest rate so you can regain control of your financial life.

Financially savvy individuals can use debt to fund wealth creation, particularly with business opportunities, property and investments. When you are looking at building your future through any of these areas be sure to learn and become informed. If you invest without researching your options you are probably better off putting your money into a fixed-term account at the bank.

Additional resource: For free expert advice, support for managing debt and setting a budget, go to:
www.nfcc.org

Learn to negotiate

It was when I was traveling through the Middle East that I saw expert bartering first hand. I was impressed with the techniques used by the stall owners, and the flexibility they had in cutting a deal. Negotiation is a great skill in your financial life, as well as in most other areas of life. Financially speaking, you do have scope to negotiate when purchasing some big-ticket items, especially cars and houses. But also think of employing negotiation skills next time you are offered a job. I recently worked with a client who had made a decision to change careers to meet work/life balance goals. After some groundwork he was offered an attractive package for a new position. While the initial offer equalled his previous job he didn't accept immediately, and agreed to a final base salary that was $10,000 more than he was expecting. With the additional income he has been able to invest in positive cash-flow rental properties, which in turn will generate further income.

While the prospect of negotiating might seem daunting at first, the more you negotiate the more confident you will become as your competence increases. Always remember that negotiation means finding a solution that is equally acceptable to both parties—everyone must be 100% happy with the final agreement. You also have to show that you are flexible, prepared to make compromises and meet the other person "halfway."

10 easy money-management tips:

1. Always shop around and compare prices. This isn't restricted to big-ticket items; even buying generic grocery items can save you money compared to named brands.

2. Be financially savvy. Try not to buy what you can borrow (think books/videos) and sell items you no longer need.

3. Pay off your credit card debt every month; this way you can utilize low bank fees and minimize high interest payments.

4. Always reconcile your bank statements so you are fully aware of fees or any errors that may occur. This is also a good way of giving yourself a monthly money-reality check.

5. Save interest on loans by reducing the term.
6. Don't be trapped by special promotions like 12 months' interest-free purchases. Make full repayments over 12 months and no interest is incurred; however, after that time, the interest starts kicking in. When signing a contract, read the fine print!
7. Always keep an emergency fund of three months' salary. This isn't a savings fund but can be used if you lose your job or are in genuine need.
8. Protect yourself with appropriate insurances.
9. Make use of free financial services offered by mortgage brokers and financial planners. Also, use an accountant. While the initial cost may seem high, the potential tax benefits certainly outweigh the investment.
10. Pay your bills on time to make use of any "early bird" discounts on offer.

Organize your career

Long gone are the days of working in the same company for 40 years. Today, we demand more from our working lives to satisfy our sense of accomplishment and define our identities. Two major ways in which you can organize your career are by redesigning how and when you work. Another popular alternative is establishing your own business. Both ideas require forward planning and organization to ensure you have a career that helps you meet your larger goals of work/life balance.

Redesign your work

You have the choice to work for an organization that supports flexibility. There are many common assumptions about flexible work—that it is only for employees with children, it's a female issue, there should be a clear boundary between work and personal life, customer service organizations can't provide these practices, and colleagues will be resentful. The reality is that at some time in their lives everyone will need to use flexible practices— to study, travel, contribute to the community, pursue an interest, care for elderly parents or a sick partner, or to spend time with their children.

While it is important for employers to recognize that creative steps are needed to make the workplace more flexible, as an individual you are ultimately responsible for the direction of your working life. Revisit the priorities and vision you established in Chapter 1, and choose a work schedule that suits your lifestyle and aspirations.

Some modern flexible work options:

- **Part-time work**—part-time workers can work under a number of different arrangements, such as working two full days a week, five half-days a week, 20 hours a week, 80 hours a month, and so on.
- **Job sharing**—this is the voluntary sharing of the responsibilities and tasks of one job between two part-time employees. Because each employee does half a full-time job, this does require a high level of communication and organizational skills.

- **Temping**—workers are employed for short periods of time, particularly in office environments, traditionally through temporary recruitment agencies.
- **Contract work**—while this type of work involves marketing yourself and a lack of security, pay can be considerably higher and the ability to choose work when required to fit your lifestyle is valued highly.
- **Flextime**—this includes "glide time," which involves staggered start and finish times.
- **Working from home**—some employees work from home while caring for a family member who is ill or to complete a project on an ad hoc basis. "Telecommuting" refers to those who always work away from the traditional worksite using remote computer access.
- **Study leave**—specific arrangements for study and exams can be negotiated with employers.
- **Career-break schemes**—reasons for career breaks can include caring for children, community activities or study for higher qualifications.
- **Phased retirement**—this can include being rehired as a consultant, working reduced hours, becoming a part-time worker or job-share arrangements. The time-frame can range from six months to five years.

While you may be attracted to one or more of the options described above, you may also be thinking, "The company I work for would never go for a flexible arrangement," or "It can't be done with my type of job." Admittedly, human resources teams need to be able to deal with flexible arrangements, support is needed from the top level of the organization and the arrangement needs to be clearly outlined for the benefit of everyone involved. Ultimately your company or organization needs to have a culture that supports flexibility, then the next step is establishing an individual arrangement.

Over a decade ago when I was in college, I negotiated a part-time role at a newspaper, so each semester I could rearrange my hours to accommodate my study. While I didn't purposely pursue a flexible work situation, I needed a part-time job that would fit around my lectures and tutorials—my primary focus at that time of my life.

While a number of employers provide specific flexible working conditions, more often than not an option like this may need to be initiated by the employee as an individual. Human resource specialists agree that the best way to approach this is with a well-thought-out, professional, written proposal. Before you begin, consider factors such as the size of the organization, the nature of its business and the existing resources. Do your homework and check existing agreements and policies. Once you have discussed and agreed upon a new arrangement, ensure you receive a letter of agreement from your employer. This is exactly what Jim, a 39-year-old father of three and senior executive, did. He has made the transition from full-time work to a 10 a.m.–2 p.m. work day as he has chosen to spend more time with his young children. He first discussed the idea with his family, as it meant a reduced income, then once the decision was made Jim approached his HR team to learn about appropriate policies.

Use this eight-step plan for creating a proposal for the flexibility you want:

1. Describe the proposed working arrangement, detailing exactly how you see it working, and clarify your availability to meet unexpected work at times when you are not scheduled to work.

2. List the benefits for your employer—they want to know how your proposed schedule will enhance your ability to get the job done.

3. List the benefits for yourself—while you want to focus mainly on the benefits for your employer, it is also important to identify the reason for your request and how it meets your personal goals.

4. Identify potential barriers that the arrangement could raise with clients and colleagues, and current options to overcome these obstacles.

5. Identify the way you will maintain contact with your office and clients. Think about how you will let others know of your new schedule.

6. Describe any additional equipment that your arrangement may require, or additional expenses. Consider the savings to the business, too.

7. Compare your current and proposed work schedules.

8. Suggest a review and evaluation process to monitor and improve your work situation.

Start your own business

Do you dream of being your own boss? Stepping out on your own can be the most exciting challenge of your working life. Are you prepared to work long hours without regular income and with no guarantee of success? This is the reality for most people who start out in business for themselves. It is especially important that your family supports and buys in to your dream when you are in start-up mode. Most small businesses don't survive beyond year three, so make sure you don't become a statistic by planning in advance.

Think about how big you want your business to grow, what resources you will need and how much money you will need to start up. What about premises, machinery and any equipment you require? Who exactly are your customers and what does your competition offer?

No matter how good you think your business idea is, before you even begin trading, prepare a business plan. Even if you think all the information is in your head, it is vital that you write down your plan to ensure you have thought of everything that needs to be done in establishing your business. When I established Aspirations Limited, I spent almost six months undertaking market research, working on our business plan, and establishing systems and procedures. Think of your business plan as a road map for your business. It will also be an important document if you are seeking funding or investment in the future. Young businesses often struggle because they underestimate the start-up costs and the time it takes to make a profit. However, if you plan diligently you will decrease your naivete and be in the best position to make solid business decisions.

Your business plan should include:

- Business objectives and vision.
- A SWOT analysis—identify your Strengths, Weaknesses, Opportunities and Threats.
- A marketing plan—identifying your potential customers, if there is a need for your product/service, identifying your competitors and your promotion strategy.
- Your start-up costs (equipment, rent, vehicles, stationery, signage, promotional material, accountancy fees, legal fees and insurance).
- Operating budgets and cash-flow projections— identify what your running costs will be.
- A business structure (sole owner, partnership or company) and plan to incorporate the business.
- An organizational plan—how will the business be structured and how many staff will you employ?
- The professional support you will need, such as an accountant, banker and lawyer.
- An exit strategy—are you planning to sell your business in 10 years, list it on the stock market or establish a franchise?

Even though I was confident in my ability to do my job, the first few months of actually running a business were a steep learning curve, having to get my head around staffing issues and a barrage of compliance paperwork.

— TRACEY, 31, EVENT PLANNER

Additional resource: Free Management Library:
www.mapnp.org/library

Increasing numbers of people are working from home, either as telecommuters or running their own businesses. A home-based working environment can provide flexibility and autonomy, and reduce travel costs and expenses. If you are running your own business, it also keeps your overhead low and provides tax benefits that your accountant can advise on. However, working from home can also be a challenge, as your home and work lives blend even further.

Some home office hints:
- Install a dedicated phone line for your work.
- Don't work at the kitchen table; use a spare room (preferably with a door!).
- Use your office only for business-related work.
- Reduce costs and filing time by encouraging email contact rather than faxes or mail.
- Ditch the messy boxes and start a filing system that will support your growing business—have a separate drawer for your home papers.
- Keep all support numbers and warranty details in one place.
- Create a way to separate home and work—even if it is only closing the door to your office at the end of the day!
- Be sure to set boundaries on distractions such as personal phone calls or friends dropping in during the day because they know you will be home.

Get organized: chapter summary

Organize your time
- Minimize time-traps
- Track your time
- Plan a realistic schedule
- Manage phone use
- Set boundaries for quiet time
- Tune into your body clock
- Trade time

Organize your daily life
- Use technology to your advantage
- Manage paper flow
- Prepare ahead of time
- Delegate
- Schedule for spontaneity and interruptions
- Make it a date!
- Be smart and multitask

Organize your space
- Clear clutter
- Put systems in place
- Have a home for everything

Organize your finances
- Establish your reality
- Be brave and budget
- Cut luxuries to save
- Automate
- Reduce debt
- Learn to negotiate

Organize your career
- Redesign your work
- Start your own business.

Chapter 3

Don't get stressed

The body never lies.

— MARTHA GRAHAM

At times life can feel like a mad race as we get caught up in an adrenaline-fueled lifestyle. With so many demands and commitments, it's no wonder we regularly feel the negative effects of stress as our lives teeter out of balance.

In *Aspirations* I explained the importance of self-care. If you want to balance your life effectively, you need to put yourself first on your "to do" list. Your personal self-care plan should include healthy-living basics like adequate sleep, regular exercise, balanced meals and a healthy attitude to eating. Learning to relax and unwind from the daily stresses of life should also play a vital part in your self-care plan. Self-care is the answer to avoiding stress and coping with the madness of daily life. In fact, as far as living a balanced life is concerned, managing stress and practicing self-care are non-negotiable.

The reality of modern living is that everyone experiences stress in some way at some time. In this chapter we investigate what causes stress, how to manage it and the importance healthy living plays in a long-term approach to work/life balance. From strategies on stress identification to nutrition, exercise and sleep, this chapter concentrates on physical health as a foundation for minimizing stress and creating balance.

Stress identification

It is important to understand that everyone experiences and handles stress in different ways. A situation that might challenge one person in a positive way might totally stress out another. In this section we look at understanding stress, identifying individual triggers, and how to put in place a personal management plan to minimize the stress you experience. Let's look first at what stress is, what its symptoms are and how it manifests in your life.

Understand stress

We have all heard of the "fight or flight" response that has been passed down to us from our ancestors. The stress response is part of our programming to prepare us for danger. Admittedly, these days we very rarely need to run for our life from a predator or hunt our food to survive. However, we now need to cope with pressurized daily lives, working long hours, commuting, arranging childcare, caring for family, studying and socializing.

Physiologically, without getting too complicated, the fight-or-flight stress response works like this. When our brain perceives a stressful situation the adrenal glands release stimulatory hormones, our heartbeat increases, glucose is supplied for energy and blood is diverted to our muscles to prepare them physically. The chemical reactions that help the body gear up for stressful situations can cause problems if they continue for too long.

Stress occurs when you think the demands of a situation exceed your ability to cope. It is your perception that makes it threatening. This is why, for example, when you are working to a deadline as a project team one person may rate the stress highly while another doesn't seem to notice it. The main difference between those who cope with stress and those who don't is their interpretation of what is happening around them and their subsequent physical and emotional response to that demand. Stress-prone people will perceive a situation to be stressful when the same situation is not perceived as stressful by another person. When you receive an unbalanced demand your body reacts both psychologically and physically. In short, your level of stress is directly related to your thoughts and whether or not you feel you can meet the demand that is being placed on you at the time.

Stress mostly gets a bad rap, but surprisingly it does have its benefits. A little stress keeps us challenged, motivated and stimulated. For example, an adrenaline rush before an exam or speaking presentation can ensure you are primed and perform well. While some stress is good, however, too much is undeniably harmful to your health.

Many people fail to act on the warning signs of stress, the symptoms of which vary from person to person and situation to situation. Physical stress symptoms can include neck ache, headaches, muscle tension, tiredness, feeling run-down, rapid heartbeat, increased speed of breathing, changes in sleeping patterns, stomach upsets, colds and infections. Emotional changes include feelings of anxiety, irritability, tearfulness, aggression, confusion and a lack of concentration. You may also notice behavioral changes like a drop in your productivity or an increase in smoking or drinking as misplaced coping mechanisms.

Recently I worked with an executive who was drinking more than she would normally. Michelle (37) was going through a particularly busy time at work, while after hours she was trying to cope with a split from her long-term partner. Stress was obviously a factor in her life, and she had begun drinking heavily to help "relax" following long days that saw her struggle with headaches and muscle tension. The first step in her stress management plan was to understand what was happening in her life, then she was able to go on and identify her specific stress triggers.

Using Michelle as an example shows that our experiences and symptoms of stress can vary incredibly. Generally, health professionals agree that there are three types of stress. As you read this, consider which stress mode you most often encounter. First, there is anticipatory stress; that is, when you worry about something that is yet to happen. For example, you might have a performance review next month and you are already anxious about the outcome. Second, there is situation stress when there is an immediate threat; for example, your car sliding out of control on a wet road. Typically, these are external pressures like an accident or bereavement. Third, there is chronic stress, which is usually experienced over a long period of time and may include stress from a difficult working environment or an unhealthy relationship.

Excessive amounts of stress, to the point of not being able to cope, can lead to mental illness including depression, which requires immediate professional medical assistance.

Action task: Think back to the last time you experienced stress and recall how you displayed it. Did you feel tense, tired or grumpy? List all the physical and emotional symptoms you experienced. Use this information to help you identify stressful situations in the future.

Look for your personal stress triggers

Once you know how your body displays stress, it makes sense to take a step back even further and identify your personal stress triggers. This is what you are actually worrying about or what is causing stress. At this point understand that you may not be able to control a situation, but you can control your response. For example, rush-hour traffic and a toddler's temper tantrum aren't going to disappear in an instant, but your stress can be reduced by managing how you respond. Like many things in life, it's mostly about your attitude!

I've seen stressed-out executives take a week off work to unwind from huge pressures, but on their return their stress levels immediately return as they haven't changed the original situation. This highlights the importance of identifying the actual trigger and not just managing their symptom. Time out of the office or away from the kids might reduce your stress levels temporarily, but it certainly won't fix the problem.

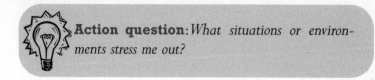

Action question: *What situations or environments stress me out?*

While not a comprehensive list, here are some common home and work stress triggers that clients regularly share with me: a demanding manager, personality clashes with work colleagues, unreliable staff, layoffs, being alone, commuting, having no social network, a health issue and disagreements in a relationship.

A recent U.S. study reported top stress triggers in this order:
1. Personal finances
2. Career
3. Too many responsibilities
4. Marriage
5. Health
6. Children
7. Loneliness
8. Sex
9. Relatives
10. Neighbors.

These are all increasingly important issues in a society where we remain single or marry later, live longer and experience less job security. But notice how many of the triggers can arise from poor communication and conflict resolution within relationships.

A major cause of stress is often the unrealistic expectations we place on ourselves. In Chapter 1, I showed you how to focus on your priorities and honor your values by aligning your goals. Don't let the busy-ness of life turn it into a competition. Working the longest hours or being the most stressed is not something to be proud of if the rest of your life is completely falling apart. Revisit Chapter 1 for more on how to scale down your expectations and prioritize what is important in your life.

Action task: Keep a stress log for two weeks. At the end of each day recall when you were stressed and what triggered the situation. Rate your stress levels on a scale of one to five. Once your log is completed, identify any patterns or trends that show your personal stress triggers.

> *I put stress into perspective. I look at whether or not it is within my control. If it is beyond my control, the stress isn't worth it! If it is within my control, I look at ways of dealing with it rather than yelling.*
> — CHARLOTTE, 28, PR MANAGER

Stress management

What if you could actually reduce stress to create more balance in your life? This isn't a trick question, because you can make the choice to manage stress. I can already hear you asking suspiciously, "Is it really possible to manage the level of stress in my life?" It's a concept that sounds almost impossible to achieve. I suggest a simple approach to dealing with your stress triggers. A word of warning— reducing and managing stress is a process; there is simply no short-term quick-fix.

While you may have identified your stress triggers, the important part of the equation is knowing when it is time to act. Learn to recognize when you are being affected by stress—those are the symptoms we looked at in the last section. Often your friends, family or colleagues may notice the symptoms of stress before you are aware of them yourself. So be quick to tune in to the feedback you receive, whether it's a caring word from a friend or a shooting pain in your shoulders as you rush to meet a deadline.

Can't find time to deal with stress? It's simple, you just have to find the time. Unless you downshift your life the stress is here to stay. And worse still, if you ignore stress it's going to build until it reaches boiling point. Something has to give. Create a saner, more balanced life by managing stress.

Hot tip: *Take slow, deep breaths when stress strikes, to help counteract the symptoms and slow your mind so you can think about your response to the situation and how you would like to react.*

In the last part of this chapter we will look at three key areas—nutrition, exercise and sleep—which all need to be factored into the stress equation. But first, let's look at eliminating the source of stress, assertiveness, relaxation and pampering yourself—strategies you can start using immediately, with immediate results.

Eliminate it!

This may sound harsh, but it's an obvious action to take—if you are stressed out, identify the source and eliminate it.

Here are some self-coaching questions you can ask yourself when you are experiencing stress:

- What is the issue or problem?
- What led to this or caused me to become stressed?
- What can I do to change or eliminate the situation?
- What is the best option for me to reduce stress?

In Chapter 2, I described the difference that clearing physical clutter can make to the management of your daily life. Now that you have cleared away the physical clutter and seen the results, it's time to think about clearing the emotional clutter that adds to your stress levels. As with your home or office, take the time to evaluate what is cluttering your mind. Ask yourself:

- What am I currently worrying about?
- Am I concerned about something specific in the future?
- What have I been meaning to "take care of"?
- Am I managing an unresolved conflict with a friend or family member?

Imagine what you could achieve if you dealt with each item. How would you spend your time and energy once the emotional clutter had been taken care of? Like physical clutter, you can choose to start either with the difficult items or with the ones that are easily checked off. Each item may involve a variety of actions, such as focusing on your aspirations, being assertive or learning new communication skills. When clearing emotional clutter, always focus on the positive outcome; that is, what you are ultimately trying to achieve. Brainstorm all the options available to you and choose a way forward that you are fully committed to. Remember, nothing will change unless you take control of and responsibility for your life. Chapter 4 includes a number of mind-body strategies that are ideal for managing stress.

The Mental Health Foundation suggests eliminating workplace stress by trusting colleagues, including everyone, giving people space, making expectations clear, appreciating good work, listening to colleagues and redistributing workloads. These ideas apply not only in the workplace but in our private lives, too.

> **Hot tip:** When facing a stressful situation or problem, don't let your anxiety get the better of you. Instead, think of five possible solutions. I guarantee at least one option will solve your dilemma.

This may all sound easier said than done, so here are some real-life examples of how to eliminate stress. Like many of us, Sarah (29) has a common daily routine that heightens her stress responses. At the end of a busy work day she returns home to prepare a meal, feed pets and manage her household. On top of this the phone seems to ring incessantly, quickly raising the stakes. Sarah has chosen a few simple ideas to eliminate stress in her evening: she now screens calls using an answering machine, occasionally buys healthy takeout and shares cooking responsibilities with her boyfriend. Sarah has been surprised at how her new calm has come about, simply by making small changes to a series of activities that previously bothered her immensely.

Maureen (34) eliminated stress in her life by arranging "back-up plans," so that when she is stuck at an appointment that has run long she can call on a friend or family to pick up the kids. With a little planning and organization Maureen can now remind herself that there's no need to worry about the kids as she has a contingency plan taking the stress out of the situation. Revisit the "build a strong network of friends and family" strategy in Chapter 1 for more ideas.

One of the most common issues we deal with in our coaching practice is clients trying to cope with the stress of an excessive workload. Before you discuss your workload with your manager, first take control by working through the action tasks in this book and committing to positive plans. Evaluate how you can manage your time better, how you can improve your flow of work, and what needs to be different for you to be able to manage the work you have. If you are taking on more work than you can actually cope with, try delegating or negotiating more realistic deadlines on your projects. If the stress you experience is mainly associated with your workload, revisit Chapter 2 for ideas on how to control the influx of information in your daily life. Use the strategies outlined to restructure your day to minimize stress wherever possible. Set new boundaries for how you interact with and relate to others.

> **Hot tip:** *Change your language to avoid perpetuating stress in your life. The next time you are asked "How are you?" don't automatically say, "Horrendously busy and massively stressed." You may think that saying this shows you are a diligent worker, but instead try saying something positive like "Great" or "Fabulous." Simply saying you are having a busy and stressful day can often be enough to evoke feelings of anxiety and panic.*

Action task: Revisit your list of stress symptoms and personal triggers. Perhaps discuss your list with a friend or colleague, and decide which stressful situations you can actively eliminate. Set compelling goals to ensure you make lasting changes.

> *I do everything that is important for the day first thing in the morning, then the stress is gone and I can relax.*
>
> — CHRISTINE, 33, TEMP WORKER

Say "No"!

Do you feel comfortable saying "No" to the requests and demands of others? You know you are not being assertive when you feel like a doormat, do something you don't want to do or are too afraid to ask for what you want. Reflect on how you react when you face conflict—are you more inclined to withdraw, be assertive or become aggressive?

Saying "Yes" is a great way of avoiding conflict with other people, but it really only adds to your own stress levels. Because it avoids conflict with other people it is often easy to justify in our minds, but what about your inner conflict? Which is more important—making others happy by saying "Yes" to absolutely everything or honoring your priorities and values by being selective? If you said "Yes" to everything, what would happen to your work/life balance? "Yes" to the volunteer work, special committees, babysitting, extra hours, social engagements—the list is endless. Learn to say "No" in a genuine and assertive way, so that your "Yes" actually means something. This way you can actively balance your needs with the requests of others, all the while reducing stress. This certainly helps toward your work/life balance, as by choosing to say "No" to tasks you can free your time to honor priorities like family and friends.

Being assertive is the ability to communicate feelings in an honest, direct, positive and tactful way. It's a great alternative to being aggressive or manipulative and an ideal communication tool to use when you need to say "No." When you behave in an assertive way you can handle disagreements and potentially fiery situations with understanding. Even when you say "No" to someone, you can still appreciate their perspective.

Five steps to assertive communication:
1. Identify the issue that is causing you stress or requires assertive communication.
2. Before you say anything, think about and decide what you would like out of the situation.
3. State your intentions, views and feelings openly and without apology. Request what you want without being pushy and demanding.
4. Listen to the other person with empathy. Identify with them and show you understand their position.
5. Negotiate to reach a mutual compromise— something that suits both of you.

Create time to slow down

In today's fast-paced world we often forget to relax. It is common for people who have lots of things to do to cram their life full of things and to get a kick out of the fact that they seem to manage it and get a stress rush. You will know that you need to slow down if the pace is affecting other aspects of your life. Maybe stress at work is leading to the breakdown of a close relationship. Perhaps your work or personal life is so hectic that you rarely prioritize your well-being, leaving you run-down and prone to illness. To live a balanced life and reduce stress it is vital that you create time to slow down, no matter how demanding you think your life is.

The key to creating time in which to slow down is to find the relaxation techniques that work best for you and fit your lifestyle. Just because your best friend swears by dawn beach walks doesn't mean this is ideal for you; you might prefer evening yoga sessions. Relaxation takes many forms; some of the more obvious ones are exercise, reading, listening to music and walking. My research showed that 38% of survey respondents regularly take time out to relax, which might include a warm bath, deep breathing, massage or meditating. Finding a mere 10 minutes a day to sit, close your eyes and simply do nothing can have a profound impact on your ability to cope with stress. Many of my clients have chosen to set aside some time every day to center their thoughts, either first thing in the morning, in the evening or by escaping at lunch time to a nearby park. One client told me that after driving home after work, and before going inside, he sits quietly in the car listening to a jazz CD for 10 minutes of solitude before switching to his home mode. Another escapes from a hectic work day before the stress reaches boiling point, retreating to the bathroom to sit for 10 minutes, focusing on her breathing. She often uses this time to focus her energy before giving important presentations, while everyone else is madly rushing around making last-minute amendments. Whether you opt for meditation or a brisk walk, solitude is essential for surviving stress.

> **Hot tip:** *Tune into your favorite sounds. Music is highly accessible and there is evidence that listening to music can reduce your stress levels.*

Of course, taking a vacation is the ultimate way to relax and recharge. It's not terribly difficult to convince most of us to take a vacation. If it came down to the wire and you had to choose between a stress-induced hospital visit or a vacation, which would you choose? You really cannot afford to be too busy to relax.

Whether your idea of a vacation is camping in a tent, five-star luxury, an action adventure or lounging with a juicy novel, have fun with your family and friends. I recently read some U.S. research that suggested people who took regular vacations had a lower risk of dying from heart disease. That's the best incentive I've heard yet for taking your annual leave!

Plan-ahead vacation tips:
- Book your trip in advance, to access good deals and a variety of choices.
- Pack light—I live by the rule of putting out everything I'd like to take then halving it. Even then I can return from a vacation with unfolded items. If you forget to pack something, either

make do with what you have or, if you
desperately need it, buy or borrow it.
- Be flexible. Something will go wrong, whether
it's a delayed flight, missed connection, double
booking, bad service or the effects of a
questionable meal. Remember the adage: you
can't change what has happened but you can
control your response.
- The purpose of your vacation is to relax and
recharge, so don't overbook yourself. Even if
you are on a hiking or cycling adventure, factor
in downtime to recover.
- If you are planning an active vacation, put a
training program in place well in advance. A few
years ago my parents Trish and Kerry walked the
scenic but strenuous Milford Track. They trained
for weeks with full backpacks and in the boots
they were to wear for the hike. When it came
to the hike they were fit and well prepared,
which made the experience much more
enjoyable.
- A favorite tip of mine is to arrive home at least a
day before returning to work so you can unpack
and ease back into your routine.

After my first long-haul international flight I suffered
terribly from jet lag. Jet lag can put a real dampener on
your vacation if you let it. Here are a few tips I have picked
up along the way that help reduce the stress of travel:
- As soon as you get on the plane set your watch
to your destination's time and sleep as you

would in your new time zone.

- Eat lightly, drink plenty of water to avoid dehydration and stretch regularly.
- When you arrive, take a gentle walk and stay awake until it's bedtime in your new time zone. Resist the temptation to take a quick snooze. Once, I arrived in Tahiti direct from London at lunch time local time and decided to have a five-minute nap—I didn't wake up till 7 a.m. the next day!
- To help cope with the time differences during a recent trip to the United States, the week before flying I started gearing up my body clock by adjusting my hours of sleep by an hour each day to make a smoother transition.

While most of us receive just two or three weeks of paid vacation a year, we simply cannot live our lives in overdrive waiting for this time. Introduce daily habits that will let you relax and recharge. Here's a list of daily relaxation favorites I've compiled from clients:

- Gardening
- Taking a bubble bath
- Aromatherapy
- Massage
- Meditation and breathing (see Chapter 4 for a "how to")
- Taking a walk in the fresh air to reduce anxiety
- Yoga
- Going for a run in the park.

Action task: Draw up a list of 10 ways you like to unwind and relax. Look at how you can incorporate at least one relaxation technique in your daily routine.

By slowing down and remaining calm I achieve a lot more by the end of the day.
— KARYN, 39, MOTHER/STUDENT

Pamper yourself

Pampering yourself is luxury relaxation at its best. When you take time to slow down you will soon see the stress-minimizing benefits that help generate balance in your life. Take your self-care to the next level and pamper yourself as often as you can. Try a home spa for the ultimate in pampering. This strategy isn't just for women—males can certainly benefit too (if you are still not convinced, I have an alternative idea—the chill-out day).

Many of my clients have adopted the home spa as an inexpensive and relaxing way to pamper themselves regularly. Creating a spa at home is easy. All you need to do is reinvent your bathroom as your exclusive pampering zone. Decide how much time you can devote to your home spa—either a morning, afternoon, evening or full-day spa. Stock up on exfoliating scrubs, face masks, conditioning hair treatments, body moisturizers and bath products. Choose from a menu of beauty therapies you can carry out at home yourself: facial, manicure, pedicure, bubble baths. For an added treat, many massage therapists offer mobile services. Create a special atmosphere with scented candles, relaxing music and plenty of plush towels. Switch off the phone and don't answer the door. Retreat to a serene time and space—an ideal stress-buster at the weekend or at the end of a busy day.

If a home spa doesn't appeal, try a chill-out day. Designate a day when you give yourself permission to relax with a good book, or clear a day of all commitments for the ultimate opportunity to indulge in spontaneity.

Pampering yourself doesn't need to be a day-long event. You can also indulge in small daily habits like a waterfront walk, alfresco breakfast or reading the newspaper over a fruit smoothie. Ask yourself what small pleasures can enrich your life on a daily basis?

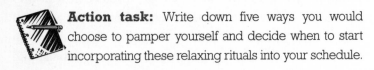 **Action task:** Write down five ways you would choose to pamper yourself and decide when to start incorporating these relaxing rituals into your schedule.

Stress and health

All the health experts I have spoken with agree that managing stress is best achieved by living a healthy lifestyle—eating well, exercising regularly and relaxing. Without a doubt, good health is the foundation for managing stress and balancing energy in your daily life.

In coaching clients on a range of issues the best guidance I can give is not to try to make too many changes at once, especially when it comes to healthy living. As you read these strategies you may be inspired and motivated to make many changes at once. You might decide to stop smoking, reduce your alcohol consumption, stop eating junk food and begin an exercise program. Pick one area to begin with and focus on it 100%. As the changes become part of your regular daily habits, build on this momentum by making another change. For example, as you increase your fitness, you can add in a healthier eating plan to ensure that your lifestyle improvements are long lasting. Just as you brush your teeth every morning without a second thought, aim to have your new healthy living habits incorporated into your daily schedule in the same way.

> *I make my health and self-care a priority, which means making time for the gym no matter how tired I feel and eating healthy foods. It also means regularly scheduling in some quiet time for myself. If life is feeling a bit tough, I try to think, "What do I need that could make this day easier?" Sometimes it's as simple as having my lunch in the sun and reading a good book.*
> — JACINTA, 33, RESEARCH CONSULTANT

Eat better

With a constant stream of new fads and celebrity diets, the world of nutrition can be confusing. Surviving for a month on cabbage and watercress soup is not a healthy, balanced ideal. Neither is an exclusive protein or carbohydrate-free diet. But as Caryn Zinn, a registered dietitian, sports nutritionist and senior lecturer at AUT (Auckland University of Technology), explains, "Eating well is not rocket science. Once you are organized with food, it is much easier to stay committed.

"If you do lose motivation along the way you just need to remember how much energy you can have when you eat properly and are well hydrated. This should be enough to keep you committed," she says.

Caryn advises people to choose healthy eating in their life now and forever. The principle is energy in versus energy out—that's managing your balance of food consumption and physical activity. Food provides fuel for our bodies, to help them perform at their best, and it starts as soon as you start your day.

"Breakfast is the most important meal of the day. It not only kick-starts your metabolism, but it can provide up to 11% of your daily fiber needs, which is a vital nutrient that most people don't get enough of," Caryn explains.

She also cites studies that show eating breakfast can help keep you more alert.

"Breakfast has also been shown to improve speed in short-term memory tests and help with problem solving. Other research indicates that breakfast is also associated with a more positive mood and lower stress levels."

Let's talk about healthy nutrition and ban the word "diet," which is dangerous and often implies going without and depriving yourself.

"Once you go on a 'diet' it is assumed that some day you need to 'come off it' and return to normal eating habits," Caryn says.

Instead, adopt lifelong healthy eating habits rather than restricting your food intake in an extreme way. While the food pyramid has undergone a major review recently, stick to the basic guidelines of eating mostly whole grains, nuts, vegetables and fruit and less bread, pasta, potatoes, processed foods, meats, sugar and alcohol. This way you can enjoy treats in moderation, although Caryn also encourages making rewards something other than food, like going to a movie or buying new clothes.

An important part of re-educating yourself to eat healthily is to be aware of when and why you eat. How often do you go to the fridge when you are sad or stressed, indulge in fast food when you need comfort, or treat yourself to a calorie-laden meal when you are bored? Overeating very seldom has to do with real hunger, says Caryn. Tune into your eating and emotional patterns so you can make sustainable adjustments to your eating.

> **Hot tip:** *When a snack-attack strikes, instead of reaching for a chocolate bar or bag of potato chips choose a healthy alternative. Keep a supply of easy snacks like dried or fresh fruit, vegetables, nuts and rice cakes on hand.*

Caryn's top nutrition tips:

- Don't skip breakfast; it's the most important meal of the day as it sets you up with energy for the day ahead.
- Eat frequently. Well-balanced small meals (every two to three hours) will give you lasting energy.
- Remember the five-plus-a-day rule—that's at least five servings of fruit and vegetables, which are the best sources of vitamins and minerals. If you are not fond of vegetables, get imaginative and dress them up with herbs, spices and low-fat dips.
- Keep hydrated by drinking plenty of water throughout the day. Dehydration can lead to fatigue and headaches.

- Avoid high-fat and refined snack foods like chips, cookies, pies, candy bars, instant noodles and crackers.
- Eat at least two or three fish meals a week. Fish is generally low in fat (especially when cooked using minimal fat!) and contains a beneficial type of polyunsaturated fat called omega 3.
- Combine carbohydrate and protein at most meals for lasting energy. For example, you might choose a salad and chicken whole-grain sandwich or a tuna salad with noodles.
- Eat low glycemic-index foods, which allow you to feel full and have sustained energy between meals. Low GI foods include whole-grain breads, rolled oats, yogurt, low-fat milk, legumes (chickpeas and dried beans), apples, stone fruits and citrus fruits.
- Exercise regularly (see next strategy); you cannot separate healthy eating and regular exercise, as both are vital for a balanced life.

Sure, this book is all about work/life balance, and I imagine many people reading this are cynical about how you can make quick and easy healthy meals. Revisit the strategies in Chapter 2 on organizing yourself, and plan your weekly shopping trip, complete with meal menus if necessary. A personal mission of mine is to make healthy evening meals in less than 20 minutes. While I enjoy experimenting with more time-consuming recipes at the weekend, during the week if a meal is going to take longer than 20 minutes to prepare, I'm simply not interested.

Action task: As in Chapter 2, when you logged how you spent your time and money, keep a food diary for two weeks. Note down every morsel that passes your lips. Don't forget to include your fluid intake too. This action task will give you a reality check on what and when you are eating. You can then decide sensibly where you need to make changes. For expert advice and personalized guidance take your diary to a nutritionist.

Exercise more

Not only does exercise improve your fitness and strengthen your body, it helps you relax and cope with the symptoms of stress. Twenty-six percent of survey respondents told me that they manage stress mostly through exercise—anything from a game of tennis to yoga.

As with healthy eating, don't just exercise to lose weight, but for a fitter, healthier body. Exercise instantly boosts your mood, countering a lengthy day at work, and it has long-term benefits for your health. Exercising more can be a very real challenge, however, whether it is finding the time and money or just struggling to roll out of bed in the morning into your workout gear. Maybe you think you don't have anyone to train with, or simply don't enjoy running or going to the gym. Perhaps you have a low self-image or have convinced yourself that you are not a sporty type.

Let's first take a closer look at the benefits of regular exercise. Exercise helps you manage your weight, sleep better, improve fitness and, of course, it is the ultimate stress-buster. When you look at the medical benefits of exercise you'd be crazy not to be putting your sweats on and getting into it. Regular exercise increases your energy levels and puts you in a positive mood. Studies also show that regular exercise prevents heart disease, high blood pressure, high cholesterol and osteoporosis. For this reason, health professionals generally recommend exercising for at least 30 minutes five times a week.

While we all know the benefits of exercise, the trick to integrating fitness into your daily life is to choose something you enjoy. Make exercise an enjoyable habit rather than a chore or "must do." Choose from team sports, power walking, yoga, running or gym classes—the options are limitless. The most commonly reported obstacles to exercising include lack of time, lack of energy, bad weather and a lack of childcare. If you feel too tired to exercise, find a friend you can work out with for extra encouragement and commitment. Alternatively, work out in the morning when your energy is higher, or if you prefer to exercise after work have a mid-afternoon snack for an energy boost. If you are employed outside the home and additional childcare is a barrier for you, work out during your lunch break. Or where possible include your children—maybe stroller power-walking, or cycling with older kids—this way you are spending time together and exercising simultaneously. If you look out the window and see a gloomy day, don't let your enthusiasm fade. Find indoor options—even exercise videos and home equipment. Or invest in some protective wet-weather clothing that will make you more comfortable. If you think there simply aren't enough hours in the day to both exercise and socialize, combine activities like walking or team sports with friends.

The most obvious obstacle to sticking to a fitness plan is making time to exercise. But you can find a workout that fits into the busiest life. Try walking, cycling, swimming or running for any length of time to suit your schedule. The golden rule of fitness is that something is always better than nothing. Tailor a work-out to your mood and available time, but don't fall into the trap of thinking that if you don't have at least an hour you shouldn't bother at all. Half an hour every day is better than no exercise at all.

Leading personal trainer Stephanie McKee says those new to exercise should include some cardiovascular exercise like swimming, running, power walking, cycling, boxing, martial arts, Rollerblading or aerobics classes. Any of these can be combined in a program with resistance exercises like weights, circuit training or resistance-band activities. She also advises beginners to build their fitness over 12 weeks before they get involved in a team sport. But Stephanie's golden rule is that exercise should be fun.

"If you aren't having fun with what you are doing, you are not very likely to stick to it," she says. This may mean regularly changing the type of exercise you are doing to maintain your enthusiasm.

"Most of all, enjoy what you are doing; a power walk with friends is a good way to catch up on gossip and get fit at the same time," explains Stephanie.

While many clients see Stephanie for a weight-loss fitness program, she finds that clients achieve their fitness-related goals more quickly if they find an event like a fun run or triathlon to train for.

Stephanie's top fitness tips:

- Be realistic—a little exercise is better than none at all. Do something active every day.

- Set short-term fitness goals which will lead you to your longer-term fitness goals.
- Track your progress by recording the training you plan to do, and the actual exercise you did. Be honest with yourself.
- Losing momentum? Exercise with a friend or a trainer to get you back on track.
- Work out in the morning and you are more likely to persevere with your training program.
- Work out for 30–40 minutes at lunch time for an afternoon pick-up.

Consistency is the key to exercising regularly, as our bodies benefit from a long-term approach. Fitness specialists advise that it is always better to choose the daily 45-minute walk over the weekly one-hour run. It is important to increase your cardiovascular fitness through regular exercise, rather than placing additional stress on your body from infrequent exercise that it is not used to. If you are new to exercise or have any health conditions, see your doctor first.

There are a lot of activities you can choose from to maintain your fitness. If you like variety, mix up gym sessions with walks, runs and team sports. If you don't like working out in a gym, choose tennis, kayaking, running or anything that inspires you to get moving. However, stop and think before you commit your time and money to new activities. Have you ever rushed into a new gym membership or found yourself dreading going to a sports practice? Ideally you want a fitness plan to be something you enjoy, that is easily accessible and that fits your lifestyle. Consider your goals: do you want to increase your fitness, socialize or lose weight? Think about access and availability—do you need facilities that are available around the clock or can you manage if they are open limited hours? If you work a regular nine-to-five job and commute to work, and your gym closes at 6 p.m., it's highly unlikely that you will be able to make full use of the gym. Similarly, if you join a sports team but practice or game times don't fit your schedule, reconsider what will work.

Other easy ways to increase your daily activity are by taking the stairs instead of the lift, walking to shops, getting off the bus one stop earlier and walking, and parking the car further away from your destination. You've heard it all before, but experiment for one week and see the difference exercising makes to your mood and energy levels.

> **Hot tip:** *Always choose an activity that you enjoy and look forward to.*

Self-coaching questions:
- How do my fitness plans fit with my goals and personal priorities?
- What are my key motivators to start exercising?
- What have been my excuses not to exercise?
- What exercise hasn't worked for me in the past?
- What exercise has worked for me in the past?
- What exercise can I commit to participating in regularly?

> **Hot tip:** *Schedule your exercise and fitness workouts in your diary at the beginning of the week. Make them non-negotiable appointments that you don't miss.*

Exercise almost always puts any problems into perspective, and it means an hour (and a shower!) to yourself a day.

— SUSAN, 46, COMMUNICATIONS ADVISOR

Sleep well

Getting enough sleep is vital for healthy living. Sleep is often the missing link for achieving optimal health. It is as important as exercising and eating healthy food in the life balance equation. Sleep allows your body to rest, recover and renew itself in a far more effective way than any other de-stressor. If you aren't well rested you simply cannot perform at your best, so never compromise your sleep. Are you getting your eight hours' sleep? This is the average daily requirement, but your body may need a little more or a little less. Anything from six to nine hours is acceptable. You will know you need more sleep if you fall asleep as soon as you settle down in bed. On average, it should take 20 minutes to drift off to sleep. However, if you are still tired when you wake after a full night's sleep, discuss this with your doctor to rule out any sleep disorders or health issues. Often when you are suffering from stress your sleeping habits will be disrupted and add to your exhaustion and low energy levels. Sleep deprivation can also lead to other serious health issues.

Eight top tips to enhance the quality of your sleep:

1. Safely get regular exposure to daylight.
2. Avoid alcohol and caffeine in the evening; instead opt for a herbal drink with calming properties.
3. Wind down from a stimulating day by setting aside "quiet time" to read and relax.
4. Don't doze on the sofa in front of the TV; go to bed when you begin to feel drowsy.
5. Reduce your light levels with dimmers or turn off bright lights before bedtime to create a relaxing environment.
6. Ensure your bedroom isn't too warm, and that it is well ventilated.
7. Check that your mattress is supporting your body.
8. Frustrated by not being able to fall asleep? Try deep-breathing techniques or get up and read until you feel sleepy.

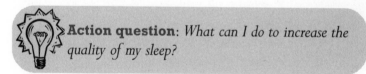

Action question: *What can I do to increase the quality of my sleep?*

Don't get stressed: chapter summary

Stress identification

- Understand stress
- Look for your personal stress triggers

Stress management

- Eliminate it!
- Say "No"!

- Create time to slow down
- Pamper yourself

Stress and health
- Eat better
- Exercise more
- Sleep well.

Chapter 4

Get connected

The mind moves in the direction of our currently dominant thoughts.
—EARL NIGHTINGALE

Metaphysics—the study of philosophy and spirituality—has led to the use of a number of techniques such as visualization, affirmations and positive thinking, that are all derived from ancient religions. While often dismissed as New Age hype, these techniques have some very practical and effective daily applications.

Just as we are all responsible for the results we achieve in our lives, it is our thoughts and attitudes that create our reality. Throughout the last three chapters you will have seen how important it is to focus on your personal priorities and aspirations. I have shown how you can increase your personal efficiency to actively promote balance in your life. Chapter 3 described further techniques for balancing life, especially in managing stress. Building on each of these concepts, we now look at your thoughts and beliefs, and the influence of metaphysics in balancing your life.

In this chapter I will present a range of simple techniques that you can adopt. You might choose to use some of these techniques to reach your goals or for relaxation, both of which will assist you in gaining work/life balance.

Connect with your aspirations

It is one thing to say what your big dreams are, quite another to fully believe in yourself and your aspirations. Visualization and intuition are two techniques that can help you connect with your aspirations. Both techniques work well alongside the ideas you discovered about your personal priorities and goals in Chapter 1. Continually revisit your vision and life purpose to inspire you to keep working toward your ideal work/life balance.

Visualize your success

Elite athletes visualize themselves crossing the finish line or winning a game. Similarly, actors auditioning for a part often imagine themselves as the character they are playing. Business entrepreneurs also picture their ventures being realized. If you can't visualize an important achievement in your life, it simply won't happen.

Visualization is a practical technique that can be easily incorporated into your routine. Simply picture yourself living your dreams. This will help you focus on the actions you need to take to reach your aspirations.

When you practice seeing yourself in a situation, it becomes more real in your mind. Whether you choose to visualize yourself gaining a hard-earned promotion, scoring well in an exam, presenting a new project or relating with others better, start seeing yourself as you want others to perceive you. You can use this technique for virtually any work/life balance issue or goal.

Find a few minutes every day, whether it is a quiet moment before your day begins, in the shower, while eating a meal or before you go to sleep. Close your eyes, breathe deeply, mentally play a movie of how you want a particular situation to be played out and focus on the positive outcome. This can work for an upcoming job interview or an important meeting. Outside of work, visualize spending quality time having fun with your family and friends. In your mind's eye, run through the scene, noticing how you act, look and sound. Alternatively, you may choose to mentally preview your day, visualizing what you want to achieve and handling any situation with confidence. Once you have the vision in your mind you can then work backward, through the steps that you need to take to meet your goals.

Shakti Gawain, a pioneer in affirmation and visualization techniques, advises creating in your mind a clear picture of what you want and focusing on it often in a positive way. A key element that will determine how well visualization will work for you is whether you have a great desire to have or be what you have visualized, and also your belief in your goal and the possibility of reaching it.

Another visualization technique is mirroring the behavior of your role models. In Chapter 1 we looked at the importance of role models. Now recall the most influential people in your life, and think of a situation in which you want to be more confident or that you want to handle in an assertive way. Visualize your role model dealing with the situation—even how they balance their private and public lives. Now emulate their behavior and actions in your own life. This is a powerful method of translating visualization into action which in turn leads to authentic balance in your life.

Recently I worked with Jenny (22) who was studying to be a fashion designer. She contacted me because she needed added momentum to keep on track with a demanding study schedule. As I was writing this book, she emailed me an update as she prepared to graduate. She was excited to report that not only was she graduating (she had previously doubted this would happen), she was showcased in Fashion Week and had also completed work experience with her role model, a well-known and respected fashion designer. She had visualized working with this particular designer and used the technique to help her identify the actions she needed to take to make this happen. This included balancing her studies with part-time work and family time. Visualizing also gave her a confidence boost, and working with her role model allowed her to increase her skills while she completed a research project. This is a great example of how visualization techniques can be practical and apply to everyone, both at home and at work.

There are many visualization techniques—another is for relaxation. When I was training to be a coach I was introduced to a technique called a "five-minute vacation." I have since read about many similar ideas, from "vacation visualization" to "20-minute retreats." This variation uses visualization to relax and escape the pressures of our hectic lifestyles. I like the idea of a five-minute vacation, as it's a short enough length of time for us all to find and commit to in a day. This exercise has meditative qualities by allowing you to focus on feeling rested and calm.

Follow these tips to enjoy your five-minute vacation:

- Prepare for your five-minute vacation by sitting comfortably, closing your eyes and breathing slowly and deeply for several minutes.
- Mentally take a vacation by letting yourself daydream about a favorite place. In your mind's eye focus on sensory details like the warmth of the sun, sand between your toes, water sluicing off your body, the smell of freshly cut grass, the taste of an ice-cold drink. As you do this, focus on breathing slowly and deeply. Focus on how calm and centered you feel on your imaginary vacation.
- As your five-minute vacation draws to a close and you open your eyes, hold your relaxed state of mind.

Action task: Take a five-minute vacation every day this week. Alternatively, visualize yourself being positive, confident and balancing your life, while coping with life's daily hurdles.

Trust your intuition

When was the last time you had a flash of insight, gut feeling, sixth sense or hunch? Whatever you call it, this was your intuition at work. We use our intuition almost every day, from simple decisions like what to wear to more important decisions like choosing a life partner. It can play an important part in making decisions that lead to your ideal life balance.

Your intuition might tell you when someone is lying, guide you to find the perfect gift for a friend or lead you to contact a sibling you feel needs to talk with you. Have you ever picked up the phone to call a friend just as they were dialling your number? This happened to me not long ago. Maybe you have met someone and, for no reason that you could logically explain, just felt something wasn't right about them, then went on to learn that in fact they weren't a person of integrity? Foresight is a wonderful thing, so be receptive to relying on your intuition a little more. I have also heard uncanny recollections of intuitive messages saving people from major accidents, discovering serious illness in time to receive treatment or causing chance meetings of a soulmate.

 Action question: *When was the last time I received an intuitive message and was provided with valuable information?*

Intuition isn't some kind of spooky magic at work. Intuition is an instant and immediate knowing, without knowing why you know. Sounds confusing, doesn't it? But intuition doesn't rely on hard facts and evidence. It is an extension of our sensory perceptions and a way of communicating non-verbally through feelings and sensations. Intuition complements rational thinking, and it includes the ability to read non-verbal clues, especially body language.

Another way of looking at intuition is to consider that everything you sense, remember, feel or notice has meaning for you. In this way, intuition extends your range of awareness. Learn to recognize your intuition by tuning in to your body and being completely aware. As with relaxation techniques, visualization and meditation, start by finding a quiet space, clearing your mind and focusing on your breathing. Focus your awareness on every part of your body. Next time you make a decision, notice how your body feels, from a flutter in your stomach to nausea, a racing heart, warmth or a tension release. Your physical responses are very telling, so learn to trust your body's signals and act on your intuition. From informal polling, most people have told me they feel calm, comfortable or detached when they receive intuitive messages.

Action task: To cultivate your awareness, use your senses to gather information. Close your eyes for just a few minutes and notice what you smell, hear, feel, taste and sense.

At times your intuition will be wrong, especially when you are run-down or under stress. Revisit Chapter 3 to make sure you are taking the best care of your body and managing stress. When you notice your intuition is wrong, take the time to differentiate what you felt so you can get better at distinguishing between your gut instinct and a stomach upset!

Often we dismiss our intuition when our common sense speaks up and tells us how silly we are being or that something doesn't make logical sense. I'm not suggesting you should rely exclusively on intuition when making decisions. Intuition doesn't have to replace intelligent rationale, but it can be used as an additional resource. Have the confidence to use your intuition as a tool. Trusting your intuition can allow you to reconnect with what is most important to you in life, which will lead you to finding the right life balance.

Action task: Next time you are about to make a decision that will impact on your work/life balance, connect with what you feel intuitively. Notice how a "Yes" or "No" response makes your body feel and choose the best option.

Generally our intuition is underdeveloped, as we are brought up in a culture where we are taught mainly to use hard facts to make rational decisions. For example, a CEO would be likely to be laughed at if she made important business decisions based solely on her intuition when normal protocol dictates that such decisions involve cost projections and data analysis. However, I have worked with entrepreneurs who have run with an intuitive idea, but then researched and planned their idea to make it a sound business proposition. Trust your first impressions.

Connect with your words

Whether written or verbal, our words are a primary method of communication. What you intend or imply is mostly indicated by these words when you communicate with others. The words we say or write are also powerful ways of connecting us to our priorities and balancing our lives. Be inspired by your own words, whether they take the form of a regular affirmation or writing in a journal. Consciously connect your words to your thoughts as you work toward work/life balance.

Use affirmations

Affirmations are positive statements that are regularly repeated to reinforce self-belief and instill confidence and life balance. They are a powerful way to shift your thinking and move to a positive state of mind. You can create short affirmations for any area of your life. Some examples to get you started include:

"I am relaxed and stress-free always."

"I am balancing my work and home life."

"I am focused on my personal values and priorities."

While you may initially feel silly repeating your affirmation, your subconscious mind will soon accept your new thoughts—you are, in effect, reprogramming your negative self-talk. If you ever misbehaved at school and were given lines to write in the hope of modifying your behavior, you may begin to appreciate the place of affirmations. Of course, when using affirmations today they should be positively worded statements. You can write them in your journal repetitively or say them to yourself every day to reinforce a positive attitude.

I asked popular affirmations authority Rebeckh Burns for an explanation of how affirmations actually work.

"Affirmations are power tools," she says. "They work by changing the negative chatter in your mind to be more positive. By thinking positively you attract positive results to your life.

"Why tell yourself a whole lot of bad stuff and feel down, when you can tell yourself positive things and feel good? You are what you think you are. Think 'beauty' and you will manifest beauty. If you want prosperity you can repeat this affirmation: 'I now attract prosperity into my life.' Simple, but it definitely works."

Award-winning entrepreneur Hamish Conway agrees. His story shows that you don't need to be sitting in the lotus position chanting your affirmation; he repeated his daily affirmation in the shower! You too can repeat your affirmation in the bath, while driving, in front of a mirror or while doing housework.

"I started really believing what I was saying, visualizing myself receiving the award and actually feeling those emotions. That is what probably made the biggest difference," Hamish says.

He also admits that using an affirmation gave him the motivation to complete the individual actions needed to reach his goal of being named Ernst & Young's Young Entrepreneur of the Year in 2002.

Additional resource: www.flameproducts.com

Guidelines for affirmations:

- Always say affirmations in the present tense, for example "I am . . ."
- Phrase affirmations using positive words and language.
- Avoid negative language like "I am not . . ." or "I will try . . ."
- Talk continually about what you want and not about what you don't want.
- Keep affirmations short and simple to increase their effectiveness.
- Choose affirmations that feel right for you and reflect what you are trying to achieve.

Action task: Using the guidelines above, write or choose an affirmation that you can use daily as you move toward work/life balance.

Mind your language

Choose your words carefully, as they can really make a difference to your attitude. While a large proportion of our communication is non-verbal, what you say is still important. Negative language simply reinforces a negative attitude. Imagine what positive words can do to your stress levels and sense of balance! Your choice of words can determine your frame of mind, so choose to use positive language.

First, reframe any negative language you currently use. Replace "nervous" with "excited." Disappointed? Maybe you will choose to be "surprised." The classic reframe that I hear executives use is making "problems" into "challenges" or "opportunities." Next time you catch yourself thinking or saying a negative word that may increase your perception of stress, stop and think of a more positive word to replace it with. Also eliminate words like "can't," "should" and "try." The word "try" is an especially weak word. How feeble does it sound to say "I tried to get fit," or "I'll try and meet the deadline." Instead, replace the word and commit to taking positive action. Saying "I'll meet the deadline" is far more appealing. By reframing you are changing the scene and making your vocabulary more positive. Another trick is to refer to negative situations in a way that makes them temporary. For example, if you are ill maybe you will choose to describe yourself as "recuperating." Similarly, rather than saying that you are poor and can't afford to buy what you want, maybe change your language—saying instead that your priorities are different at this time.

> **Hot tip:** When you catch yourself saying what you don't want, remind yourself to say what you do want instead.

Increasing your awareness and understanding of what you say can be a powerful tool in keeping you positive and moving forward. Also tune in to what others around you are saying, to enable more effective communication. As a coach I often listen for the communication mode that clients use. Generally, the three modes are auditory, visual or kinesthetic. We all favor a specific sense, and this is reflected in our language. For example, an auditory person might say "I hear what you are saying," a visual person might say "I get the picture," while a kinesthetic might say "Hold that thought." Knowing a colleague's or partner's preferred mode of communication can help you to make decisions together and handle potential conflict.

Action task: Record or video a natural conversation that includes you, then review it so you can analyze your own language. Identify any patterns or negative phrases you use regularly and substitute more positive language.

Write a journal

Writing is a therapeutic way of connecting with your inner thoughts and feelings, and journals provide a safe place to record your most personal concerns and desires and organize your thinking.

At a basic level there is the journal where you use bullet points and short writings to record your goals, values and mission, and to evaluate your progress. I have used this type of journal for many years and found it to be an inspiring way of collecting my thoughts. I record only positive items, so it is a very motivating diary to read and reflect on in more challenging times.

Recording your aspirations is an important part of building your own success and achieving work/life balance. The first rule of effective goal-setting is to write down your goals, so you can then evaluate and monitor your progress. Writing your goals and objectives in one place means you can easily review your intentions and record your results.

In *Aspirations*, I also introduced a daily diary format that has become popular with many clients. It includes noting down in bullet-point form the day's success or achievement, understanding or insight, question and gratitude.

A better-known type of journal is the longer format, "confidante" or "best friend" variety. A journal really is like a friend—even better, as you can write absolutely anything you want without having to worry about offending anyone. It's a safe space in which to write everything you feel without hurting anyone's feelings or being judged on your behavior—the ultimate in self-expression.

Writing can also provide a fresh perspective on life, helping you to discover the challenges that are preventing you from achieving work/life balance, and allowing you to reach your potential. If you think a journal has to be a

Bridget Jones–style ramble of cigarette, alcohol and calorie consumption, think again.

Writing a journal allows you to clarify your thoughts and feelings. It can help you identify the areas of your life that you want to improve, and find a way to make necessary changes. Your journal is the perfect place to explore your self-awareness—to discover what holds you back, find the regular patterns that get in your way, then focus on problem solving and taking action. Keeping a journal enables you to make sense of things in your life, whether it is a decision about having children, staying with a life partner, moving between cities or changing careers.

Recently I worked with John (43), who was in the process of leaving an unhappy marriage. He decided to start a diary to help rebuild his confidence and manage his feelings of denial and anger. John credits his journal-keeping with helping him keep on track with his recovery from the divorce. It was an important process in helping him adjust to his new life, and it also helped him discover how he could balance his new demands and responsibilities. He acknowledges that some of his journal entries were written when he was in crisis mode, but when he looks back on them he appreciates how much he has since developed as a person.

You too will undoubtedly grow through the process of writing, even if you start with pinpointing solutions to the challenges in your life.

To start with, try different writing styles; here are a few ideas:
- Write about your ideal work/life balance scenario.

- Write about what success means to you.
- Write a dialogue between your unfit self and the healthier self you want to be.
- Visualize your work/life balance and then record the experience in words.
- Write yourself a letter from the future when your life is as balanced as you would like it to be.
- Write a script for how you would like a situation or conflict to be resolved.
- Write a letter of forgiveness.
- Write about everything you appreciate in life.
- Write a letter to a friend explaining why you value them.
- Write about your positive qualities and attributes.
- Write about what you would do if you lived a different life.
- Write about your personal priorities for the next three months.

And a few practical considerations. Buy a special diary that you will only use for your journal. Create a regular time of solitude to devote to writing. Write about anything: your concerns, worries, desires and aspirations. Don't analyze or judge what you write, and keep it private. These basic guidelines will keep you on track and allow you to benefit from the writing experience.

Alternatives to keeping a written diary include making use of technology and recording a video or audio journal. You can even write emails to an imaginary friend. If you are visually creative, use collages or make up a scrapbook of inspiring images that represent your ideal work/life balance.

Action task: Choose the type of journal and method that suits you, and embark on a writing experience to uncover your potential and increase your self-awareness. Start by writing what benefits you would like to receive from regular writing.

> *I write in a gratitude journal every night without fail. I write only positive things, and I list at least five good things that have happened to me that day—receiving flowers, completing an essay, spending time with my dog or seeing a beautiful sunrise. Whenever I'm feeling stressed or down I remind myself what I have to be thankful for.*
>
> — JESSICA, 18, STUDENT

Write a work/life balance statement

Regardless of whether or not you choose to write in a journal, take the time to compile your own work/life balance statement. Like affirmations and visualization techniques, the principle of this exercise is to focus on what you want in life rather than highlighting the negatives. Include in your statement your ideal work/life balance, which reflects the values, goals and purpose you discovered in Chapter 1.

Here is a work/life balance statement from Jack, a 38-year-old father of three and business executive: "I choose a pleasant balance between my work and home life. I achieve my career goals with integrity, energy and honesty. My top priority is the well-being of my sons and partner. I always celebrate the success of others at home and work. My self-care plan includes daily regular exercise and healthy eating. I maintain a relaxed state of mind that encourages my co-workers and family to be positive also."

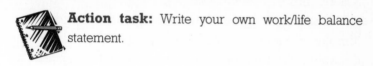 **Action task:** Write your own work/life balance statement.

Connect with your creativity

Like many people, in the past I thought that because I didn't have any natural talent for art or drawing, I wasn't creative. How wrong was I? We are all capable of being creative in different ways, such as writing, painting, cooking, photography, sewing, crafts, gardening, dancing or decorating.

Your creativity plays an important role in balancing your life, whether you are baking a child's birthday cake or wrapping a special gift. By developing your creativity you may discover better ways to do a task or uncover a hidden passion, which is why it doesn't matter if you are a lawyer, teacher, nurse, plumber and/or parent. As you unleash your creativity you will notice ways to balance your life better, simply by seeing the world in a different way.

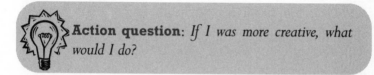 **Action question:** *If I was more creative, what would I do?*

Be inspired

Whether you tap into your creativity regularly or are new to working with it, you will need to seek inspiration.

Brilliant ideas generally don't strike you randomly, they need to be sought out. Learn to identify what inspires you and tap into this connection.

Recently I spoke with leading industrial designer Monika Conway, whose career is all about being innovative. "Inspiration comes from everything around us in the environment; it's good to feed your senses and constantly surround yourself with visual stimulus," she says. "Everything and everyone can be inspiring, including fashion, culture, art and food. You may stumble upon different ideas or look at things from a fresh perspective."

Action task: Take 10 minutes to daydream about nothing in particular. Where do your thoughts lead you? Then consider what inspires you—is it news, movies, fashion, art, food, culture, the 1930s, the 1980s, ancient history, conversations, interesting people or nature?

Shake up your routine

Creativity can't be structured or forced as you rush to meet a deadline or put pressure on yourself to come up with a brilliant idea. It is highly unlikely that you will be inspired if you have a repetitive routine day in, day out. Stimulate the creative right-hand side of your brain by shaking up your routine. Start with small changes like driving a different way to work, trying something new or going for a walk.

"You are sure to have a bunch of good ideas if you take a break, get outside and look at things a different way," explains Monika. "I often change my scenery. At work, home or in the park I feel different in each space, so obviously you can think differently too."

Monika says we can all unleash our creativity by sitting up and noticing everything around us, pushing our own boundaries and challenging ourselves to do things that are not routine.

Write yourself creative

Earlier in this chapter I introduced you to the idea of writing a journal. A journal is also a powerful way of unleashing creativity. In her international bestseller *The Artist's Way*, Julia Cameron suggests writing three pages every morning when you wake. Writing every day will open your mind to new creative ideas which you can use in other areas of your life.

An alternative to writing pages of thoughts is to mind-map, using words. In the late 1960s Tony Buzan launched the concept of mind-mapping, which many of us now use at work, home and study. It's a graphic technique that uses words, images and colors to add information and ideas to a key word as we think laterally. While it facilitates creativity it can also assist in problem solving and has excellent applications in organizing, communication, planning and note taking. You can learn more about this technique from Tony's mind-mapping books, or at www. mind-map.com.

The easiest way of using words to harness your creativity, however, is by brainstorming. "I use brainstorming as a tool for almost everything," Monika Conway notes.

While mind-mapping connects ideas and thoughts together, brainstorming is a way of collecting every and any idea regardless of whether it will end up being used.

For this process to be useful, it is important to collect as many ideas as possible and to list everything, even if it sounds ridiculous. A crazy idea may later form a platform on which to build another more useful idea. As you brainstorm ideas, either alone or in a group, focus on quantity not quality.

"You should never get stuck on the first idea, even if it seems to be the best one; you have to explore all the options," Monika reiterates.

Keep a creative scrapbook

You don't need to be an aspiring painter or writer to keep a creative scrapbook of ideas. You have probably had the experience of taking clippings from catalogs or magazines for future reference, then finding when you look for them later that they are totally lost. If, however, you paste images into a scrapbook, you can bring all your ideas together and use them for brainstorming. Or you might choose to start an ideas folder, where you can file newspaper and magazine articles for future inspiration. In Chapter 2, I suggested keeping a notebook on hand to help with your organization, and you can also use this to jot down ideas when you are inspired.

Action task: Using images and clippings, create a collage representing your life. Only add a picture to your collage if you are willing to take action to make it a reality. This action task is ideal for boosting your creativity and focusing on your ideal balanced life.

Connect with your thoughts

In *Aspirations*, I introduced the idea of limiting beliefs and how they can affect our lives. As Norman Vincent Peale famously said, "Change your thoughts and you change your world." We do become our thoughts in a sense. If you are focusing on success you will undoubtedly seek out opportunities to realize your success. Conversely, focus on the negative and chances are it will manifest in your life. So often I hear clients say their lives are unbalanced, when after making some small changes they simply need to change their thoughts and attitudes to truly appreciate their new balanced lives.

While acknowledging your thoughts is important, believing in yourself and developing a positive attitude is vital. Later we will look at meditation, a technique that can be used to combat stress and develop a positive attitude as you work toward your ideal work/life balance.

Listen to yourself

I have already mentioned how important self-awareness is. It is impossible to make changes to achieve balance in your life if you are not aware of your current situation. For this reason self-awareness, or simply listening to yourself, is the first step toward making improvements in your life. Actively listen to both your positive and your negative internal chatter. For example, if your internal voice is telling you that you are stressed, listen to it and choose how to manage the stress. Similarly, if you are working late at the office but your voice is telling you to go home and be with your partner—listen, then act. Tune in to your intuition. Again, meditation can help if you find it difficult to pick up on your own messages.

Believe in yourself

If life was as easy as having big dreams and setting your goals, as outlined in Chapter 1, everyone would be doing it and living their wildest dreams. For your dreams to become a reality you need to believe in yourself 100%. Self-limiting beliefs serve as obstacles that stop you moving forward in life. It is quite common for my clients to reel off a litany of beliefs about themselves like, "I'm not qualified," "I don't know how to do that," "It's far too hard," or "It's too late to start again from scratch." Again, self-awareness is vital if you are to identify your limiting beliefs, then you can start the process of overcoming these beliefs so you do believe in yourself.

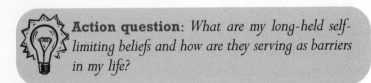

Action question: *What are my long-held self-limiting beliefs and how are they serving as barriers in my life?*

When I was researching *Aspirations* I met a librarian who told me she had always wanted to be a freelance writer. Being a coach, I asked her what she had done to realize her dream, and she told me that five years previously she had sent one unsolicited article to a magazine. Some time later she received a "Thanks, but no thanks" rejection letter. She took this sole rejection very personally, began to believe that she wasn't a good writer, and literally gave up on her dream. Having worked as a journalist I was aware that the reality could have been very different. There could have been various reasons for her rejection; for example, that a very similar article had recently been published or was already planned for the future. None of these reasons was necessarily a reflection on her ability as a writer. She could have asked for feedback on her article, or approached other magazines. Even if she was not a polished writer, she could have improved her skills by joining a writers' group or taken community classes to improve her skill base. A small dose of self-belief could have drastically changed the outcome of this woman's dreams.

Action task: Identify any negative thoughts that you perceive as limiting or blocking your progress toward your ideal work/life balance. Challenge your beliefs by identifying new beliefs that you will need to support your ideal scenario.

Adopt a positive attitude

A positive attitude will help set you up to succeed in every area of your life, including work/life balance. While being positive won't make you immune from life's tragedies, it will certainly reduce your stress levels and help you remain level-headed and centered at difficult times. There are many things you can do to develop and maintain a positive attitude. We have already looked at affirmations, which are extremely useful for building positive self-talk. Similarly, visualizing your success can be very beneficial for keeping positive. Surrounding yourself with positive people and looking to role models is another idea. Whatever you experience in life, always be willing to take away a lesson or learning experience. As expected, your self-care basics and health are also a priority when it comes to building a positive attitude. Taking action of any kind always boosts positivity too. The much-used Nike slogan "Just do it" sums up this approach.

To help condition your new attitude, next time you are in a difficult or frustrating situation, instead of asking in despair, "Why me?," focus on the positive aspects of the situation. I'm sure you have been told many times that every cloud has a silver lining, so replace a negative attitude with a positive frame of mind at every opportunity.

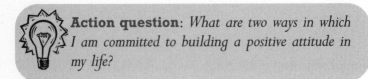

Action question: *What are two ways in which I am committed to building a positive attitude in my life?*

Meditate

Do you find your life is so busy that you can barely hear yourself think? Meditation may be the perfect mind-body technique to increase your awareness and help you balance your life. Almost every religion includes meditative practices such as repetitive praying or chanting. For this reason, there are many stereotypes surrounding meditation. Put aside any preconceptions you may have and see how you can use one of the many forms of meditation in a practical way in your own life. While meditation has traditionally been used in a spiritual context, it is increasingly being used for relaxation, unleashing creativity, developing intuition, stress management and work/life balance.

Meditation is a state of deep physical relaxation combined with mental alertness. How many times have you heard someone say how important it is to live in the moment? Being present in the moment can improve the quality of almost everything you do as you focus your full attention on every aspect of what is happening. Meditation can help you achieve this.

Common types of meditation include breathing, repeating a mantra, and action meditation, all of which share common elements.

> **Hot tip:** Don't worry about meditating properly, as there isn't strictly a "right" way. Focus your attention on your breath and be fully aware of your body.

Breathing is something we take for granted. For many years, as I battled a health condition, I was constantly told to "relax and breathe." It wasn't until five years ago, when I was physically shown how to breathe deeply into my diaphragm, that I understood the benefits. When we are under pressure we often take short, shallow, rapid breaths. Consciously take long, deep breaths in meditation. In its simplest form this can mean inhaling for a count of six, deep into your belly, feeling it rise as you inhale, then exhaling for a count of six. You can set aside time specially to focus on your breathing, or you can practice it when you are waiting for an appointment or stuck in traffic (keep your eyes open!).

Using a mantra or phrase as a point of focus in meditation is another option. Think of a meaningful word or short phrase to use as your mantra. "Om" is a common mantra, but you can choose anything. As you continually repeat your mantra, let any stray thoughts slide away. You will probably find it difficult to quieten your mind at first, but continue and you will soon feel more centered.

Believe it or not, there is also a form of meditation where you focus your attention on everyday activities like walking, showering or flossing your teeth. As discussed in the strategy for intuition, take the time to be aware of all your senses as you carry out the task slowly and rhythmically.

Guidelines for meditating:
- Find a comfortable place to sit.
- Eliminate as much distracting noise as possible.
- Sit quietly and let your mind grow still, focusing on your breathing or mantra.
- Practice once or twice daily.
- Start with 10–15 minutes and increase to 20 minutes per session.

And for the skeptics, research from Harvard Medical School has concluded that meditative deep breathing has many health benefits, including reducing blood pressure, relieving muscle tension, reducing stress and boosting immunity.

You may have many seemingly valid reasons why you can't meditate. Clients often tell me they are easily distracted and simply can't sit still. However, you can experiment with the many forms of meditation until you find a technique you like. Gemma, a 38-year-old accountant, swears by her daily meditation, although she wasn't always so keen, believing her life was far too busy to meditate. Now she spends 20 minutes a day quietly meditating as she eats her breakfast, savoring every mouthful. By the time she arrives at work she is feeling calm and centered, and is able to cope with the demands of her job.

Get connected: chapter summary

Connect with your aspirations
- Visualize your success
- Trust your intuition

Connect with your words
- Use affirmations
- Mind your language
- Write a journal
- Write a work/life balance statement

Connect with your creativity
- Be inspired
- Shake up your routine
- Write yourself creative
- Keep a creative scrapbook

Connect with your thoughts
- Listen to yourself
- Believe in yourself
- Adopt a positive attitude
- Meditate.

Chapter 5

Get going

To accomplish great things, we must not only act, but also dream, not only plan, but also believe.

— ANATOLE FRANCE

Most of this book has explored the meaning of work/life balance, looking at ways in which you can identify what is important in your life and how you can organize for balance. Managing stress, health and your attitude are vital, but in this chapter I encourage you to start taking action and learn techniques that will help you make sustainable changes.

You might have the best plans and intentions for your work/life balance, but this chapter shows you how to transform your life even further. To really get going, reach your goals and achieve balance you will need momentum and accountability. Here are 17 strategies to help you go for it, go hard and go for gold!

 Quick quiz: Have you got what it takes?
- Do you find it easy to take the first step toward your goals?
- Do you consciously project confidence even when you are not feeling as self-assured as you would like?

- Are you sure that how you present yourself to others represents who you are?
- Are you flexible and easily adaptable when it comes to making changes in your life?
- Do you find it easy to maintain momentum once you have begun to make improvements in your life?
- Do you always push through potential barriers like procrastination?
- Do you face your fears and insecurities head-on rather than letting them limit your progress?
- When you reach obstacles in your action plans are you determined to keep on striving for your dream?
- Do you regularly evaluate how you are balancing your life?
- When you seemingly "fail" do you look for ways to improve your performance or modify your behavior?
- Are you consistent in your efforts to develop your life?
- Do you plan and prepare before you take action?
- Do you have well-developed communication skills that allow you to build rapport with others and show empathy?
- In what matters most to you, are you fully committed to your intentions?
- Do you celebrate life's transitions and your personal accomplishments to further motivate yourself?

Score: Did you get a perfect score and answer "Yes" to every question?

A top score of 15 means you certainly have what it

takes to ensure you achieve sustainable balance in your life. A few "No" answers just means you need some fine-tuning. If you answered mainly "No," luckily there are some good ideas here that will inspire you to build up your personal energy reserves. Regardless of your score, pick and choose from the following strategies that will help you get going in life.

Go for it!

At times we all need a helping hand to take the first few steps toward our goals and boost our confidence. In this section we look at how you can get started by implementing your goals and making adjustments to your life. It includes fundamentals like taking the first step, boosting your confidence and being yourself. It also introduces the need for flexibility and adaptability as you progress through your goals and life cycle. In this way you can increase your enthusiasm for your aspirations and begin to achieve the balance you have been looking for.

Take the first step

Taking the first step toward work/life balance can be easy for some people and the hardest thing imaginable for others. However, your first step is pivotal in creating balance. It will help build your momentum to take the next step, and soon you will be achieving what you imagined.

At the outset, reaching your goal of life balance can seem overwhelming when you are facing so many options and tasks. You can start by listing every possible option and then prioritize the actions in some kind of logical order. Break down your large goal into small goals, even mini-sized goals, to make it easy to achieve each task. Use mind-maps, flow charts or manage your goal and its action steps just as you would manage a work project.

> **Hot tip:** *Brainstorm all the options for possible first steps toward your goals and work/life balance, then select your favorite. Let your intuition guide your choice.*

Sometimes, though, you may have a dream or goal but truly do not know where to start. This is where doing your homework through research and investigation plays an important role. For example, if you want to work from home, before approaching your manager you will need to research company policies and possible options to make this a reality. Want to get fit? Maybe you need to explore your fitness options before you begin. Embarking on a career as a chef? Talk to a chef you admire and gain advice on the best professional courses. Generally, most goals require planning and preparation, which can be a natural first step in the right direction. Ask yourself, "What information do I need to help make this decision? Where will I gather the information I need? What new skills and knowledge do I need to gain or develop?"

Taking the first step doesn't necessarily mean starting from the beginning. Sometimes it can mean starting in the middle—what is important is taking at least one small step forward. Jeremy (27) wanted to change his career as part of his work/life balance plan. He didn't know where to start, but he knew he would need to retrain and find a new job. Instead of starting by investigating training courses, he decided to attend a networking meeting of the professional association for his new career. He chose this option as a first step to inspire him to connect with others in his new profession (possibly finding a mentor) and learn from their experiences. This gave him added enthusiasm and increased his confidence to then enroll in classes and put in place other plans for his transition.

When you are ready to take the first step toward your goal, it is most important to make it a small, achievable action that will build your momentum and inspire you to continue. If you want to enroll in further study you may need to first make a phone call, send an email, visit the library or surf the Internet. If you want to make changes in your career you might take a first step by joining a professional organization, talking to others, clearing your desk or creating a new file. Whatever your first step, keep it simple and easy so you will be inspired to keep going. Be specific and make sure you are clear on the exact details of what you are going to do. Don't think for one moment that the first step needs to be a large hurdle. You don't need to go from standing still to 100 miles per hour in three seconds flat. Give yourself a break and motivate yourself using this strategy.

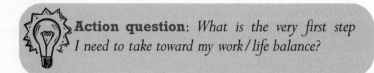

Action question: *What is the very first step I need to take toward my work/life balance?*

Action task: Revisit the work/life goals you formulated in Chapter 1 and write up a list of all the possible first steps. From this list choose one small step and move forward by implementing at least one action per day or week, whichever is most appropriate.

Fake it till you make it

Often we need an extra boost of confidence to reach our aspirations. The most powerful way to make any change in your life is to act as if that change has already occurred. Faking it till you make it is the best tip I've ever heard! Like the positive influence of affirmations on your state of mind, if you pretend to be confident for long enough, you will be. Once you start seeing yourself in this way, behaving more confidently will become a lot easier. Use the visualization techniques discussed in Chapter 4 to help you prepare for this strategy. Then hold your head up high and fake it the next time you make a presentation or go for an interview.

Of course, I'm not suggesting that you should be dishonest. But if you want to reach a certain goal you will need to express strength and confidence, which are things we all lack at times.

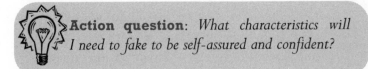

Action question: *What characteristics will I need to fake to be self-assured and confident?*

Brand yourself

Advertising and marketing executives cleverly brand products so they are instantly recognized. Branding is something that applies to us as individuals too, whether it is a high-school dropout wanting to brand him or herself for the working world, a mother re-entering paid employment, or anyone changing careers. Many people flinch at the idea of considering themselves as a "product," but consider why people sometimes don't understand or appreciate you. Maybe it is because how you look and act doesn't fully reflect the real "you." There is no point in branding or reinventing yourself if the "new you" doesn't reflect what you want. Typically your reinvention will stem from your goals and life mission.

Confidence is critical in branding. An exaggerated example is pop icon Madonna, who presents a "new and improved" version of herself every few years. Considering that most of our communication is non-verbal (55%), the way you dress, act and sound is important. This isn't about being a fashion victim, supermodel or style guru, but adapting to change and keeping modern. Remember that we make lasting impressions in the first 30 seconds of meeting someone, so it is important to measure up. Give yourself an image audit, and enlist the help of friends or professionals to update your make-up, grooming, hair and clothing.

Five steps to brand yourself:
1. Evaluate your current image. Consider asking close friends or colleagues to recall their first impressions of you. See if their answers match how you want to be perceived.
2. Identify what message you want to communicate with others through your image (for example, professional, modern, traditional, casual, etc.)

3. Analyze how your current brand is different from how you want to be perceived.
4. Identify what you can realistically do to "fill the gap" in perception.
5. Set SMART goals and action tasks to reinvent yourself in line with your values.

And when you have confidently formed your personal brand—use it! We all need to promote and sell ourselves. Despite any reluctance we might feel—the cultural cringe factor—we can all use our brand in career prospecting, meeting new people and enjoying life.

Be natural and enthusiastic

While I encourage you to "fake it till you make it" and promote your personal brand, it is vital that you are still yourself. Don't try to be someone or something you are not—honor your personal priorities and values.

Do you know why I am often told I'm a natural and enthusiastic public speaker? It's undoubtedly because I am 100% passionate and believe in what I'm talking about. That is certainly something you can't fake! Catch yourself being "you" and think about what makes you feel natural and enthusiastic.

Be flexible

Being adaptable and flexible are important qualities when it comes to improving your life. Basically, if you are trying to make changes in your life and what you are doing is not working, you need to change your approach till you get it right. Consider whether there is a better and more effective way of reaching your goal or completing a task. Later in this chapter I will outline effective evaluation strategies to help you modify your actions and behavior. In short, you need to measure your results, do more of what is working and less of what is not. There will always be more than one way to achieve what you set out to do.

Don't ever think of yourself as a failure, but use "mistakes" as learning experiences and don't make the same mistake twice. That is the best lesson of all.

It is important to be open-minded in this approach as situations themselves change, and new opportunities arise. With increased awareness you will have the ability to notice opportunities and, more importantly, with an attitude of flexibility and adaptability you will be able to act on them.

In a broader sense, we need to be flexible and adaptable as we move through our life cycle. What was your life like 10 years ago? Or even just six months ago? Life is continually changing and you need to be prepared to accept transitions in life, whether it is leaving college, starting a family, beginning a new relationship, ending another or starting a new career.

> *I endeavor to make quick decisions about trivial things so that I only have to touch them once and have more time to spend on meaningful things.*
> — TIFFANI, 34, MEDICAL STUDENT

Go hard

Now let's look at how to keep going and maintain momentum. This includes overcoming procrastination and extending your comfort zone. As we all know, while we may have the best intentions, it's the keeping on that can often be the hardest part in our pursuit of life balance. Here are some practical tools for seeking feedback so you can continually improve your performance at home and work. There are tips on perseverance, and I also explain the vital process of change in more detail.

Maintain momentum

It is easy to be upbeat when your professional and personal lives are both going well, but it is also important to keep motivated when you are faced with challenges. To maintain momentum and overcome any obstacles as they present themselves, ask for extra support if you need it and continue to let yourself be inspired by your big dream.

We have already talked about taking small first steps, the beginnings of building momentum. But once you have impetus you need to continue and carry through on your intentions. Stay on track by using your choice of the strategies discussed in Chapter 4, including visualization, affirmations and journal-keeping. In Chapter 1 we discussed the options of coaching, *Stop Living Your Job, Start Living Your Life* motivational groups and supporting others. Revisit all these strategies for maintaining momentum.

Every action you take will give you momentum and lead to some kind of result—either negative or positive. Some actions will lead you closer to your goals, while others will send you in the wrong direction. In my opinion the best way to maximize motivation and build momentum is to focus your energy on your top priority. It's as simple as that. Think about it—if you don't have the life you want it's because what you are doing is giving you the wrong results.

When I am working with clients, often just a quick weekly follow-up provides them with enough momentum to keep on achieving. If you are not working with a personal coach you can evaluate your own progress, as outlined in a strategy later in this chapter. Based on clients' success stories, the secret of maintaining momentum is to keep taking manageable, "bite-sized" steps. Sure, visualize and focus on the ultimate outcome, but when it comes to daily actions, break it down and keep it simple. Recently I worked alongside 36-year-old Elizabeth, who was working incredibly long hours to the detriment of her young family. She had a desire to switch to a career in real estate, but couldn't comprehend where she could possibly find the time to study and make the transition while managing her already hectic life. We focused Elizabeth on small daily tasks that she could easily incorporate into her life, and reviewed her time management and working habits to make her more effective. She also realized she was taking on the majority of responsibility at home, and enlisted additional support to enable her to continue to take small steps toward her larger life goals.

Similarly, with a young baby at home, 29-year-old Shannon was excited but overburdened while establishing her own business. Faced with the business start-up, promoting her business and finding clients, she was finding it hard to keep her enthusiasm and energy levels high.

Every day she took a small step in the direction of her business vision. Sometimes this step would be as small as making a phone call or attending a meeting. She maintained momentum by also meeting twice a month with a mentor and using simple evaluation techniques to keep on track. Within months her business was up and running and she had met her target number of clients.

 Action question: *What single strategy do I need to commit to 100% that will keep me on track with my goals and work/life balance plan?*

Overcome procrastination

You know you have been procrastinating when there is an item on your "to do" list or something niggling at the back of your mind that you have been meaning to do but keep avoiding. Procrastination is simply postponing action or putting things off, and everyone battles with it at some stage.

When you think about it, you can understand why we procrastinate when we have increased demands competing for our attention, which inevitably means putting some things off. Perhaps the items you are putting on the back-burner are not adding meaning to your life? This highlights the importance of defining your personal priorities, goals and values, as outlined in Chapter 1.

Procrastination keeps you looking to the past about the things you "should have done yesterday," when to reach success and create balance in your life you need to be closing the gap between where you are now and your future. Procrastinating can also lead to further stress and anxiety as you rush to meet last-minute deadlines.

I use a four-point plan for helping clients work through procrastination. First we identify what the issue of procrastination is, then we explore the reason for not taking action, options for solutions and the commitment to action. For example, Sam (31) was working toward a long-term goal of financial security which included many short-term actions such as regularly balancing his personal checking account. When questioned, he reasoned that he didn't really want to know his current financial situation as he knew he wouldn't be happy with his spending habits. He listed a number of potential options for action, including ignoring the problem, using a personal money management system, getting someone else to manage his accounts or just facing up to the fact that he wasn't making the progress he wanted. After evaluating each option he decided to deal with the issue by setting up a system to help him manage his money. By taking positive action he was able to overcome his procrastination and begin to make real changes.

Unfortunately, procrastination is the best way of putting a stop to your progress and will see you walking backward, away from a balanced life. Do not allow yourself to accept any excuses for not taking action now. Remind yourself that this moment right now is the best time to stop procrastinating. Every time you are struck by pro-crastination, remember the Nike slogan and "Just do it."

Test out the "do it now" concept and see if it makes any difference. If it gives you the momentum you need, keep it up. I guarantee that by taking some kind of action you will keep moving forward. If telling yourself to go for it doesn't provide you with enough impetus, start exploring why you are procrastinating so you are able to move out of the negative cycle of thought. Sometimes we procrastinate because we are unsure of how to do a particular task. Find a way around this obstacle by learning the skills you need or asking someone to show you how to do it. This will certainly help you beat the urge to put it off.

This may sound blunt, but if you are simply procrastinating because you don't like what you have to do, then don't do it. Ask yourself why you are doing it in the first place. Sure, you may have to do duties on the job that aren't particularly inspiring. In that case, focus on how important the task is in reaching your ultimate goals, or just get it out of the way quickly so you can spend more time on the parts of your job you enjoy. For a boost of motivation, consider how you can inject some fun into the more mundane activities you need to do. Be inventive when looking at your personal procrastination list—can you delegate it? Pay someone to do it for you (the relief of not having to do it may outweigh the expense)? Or consider automating a task using technology.

> **Hot tip:** *Don't let your fear masquerade as procrastination, especially unreal fears. Most things we fear in fact never happen—studies have shown that 90% of what we worry about never actually materializes.*

If you are continually procrastinating over a particular activity or task, be honest with yourself and ask, "What am I waiting for?" Be strong and force yourself to sit up and recognize the price you pay for stalling. Maybe you'll miss a deadline, lose a contract, miss catching up with friends, miss a promotion or end up with below-standard work. Ultimately, procrastination means missing opportunities!

Understand that procrastination is not just a harmless habit, but an attitude that stifles personal and professional growth. I once read that the difference between someone with dreams and someone who has realized their dreams is that the latter has taken action. It certainly is the key to accomplishing anything in life, so avoid procrastination at all costs.

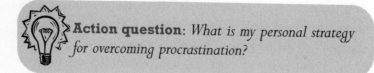

Action question: *What is my personal strategy for overcoming procrastination?*

Top tips to beat procrastination:
- Line up all the information or materials you will need in advance to visually remind you to start.
- To avoid being distracted, clear your desk of everything except what you need to complete.
- Develop a clear vision of how you will feel once you have completed the task.
- Look for three to five small tasks you can initiate quickly to create momentum.
- Tell yourself you will only work on an activity for five minutes; once you start you may not want to stop.
- Find a partner or friend who will help you get started and work alongside you.

- Share your deadlines with your support team for extra motivation.
- Don't take yourself too seriously or demand perfection.
- Get set for some challenges. Set yourself a personal contingency plan to manage potential setbacks.
- Tackle the hard bits on your "to do" list or the most difficult part of a project first. Other tasks after this will seem much easier.
- Think of a different method to complete the task more quickly.
- Reward yourself so you keep motivated and to stop you falling back into your old mind-set. Rewards don't need to be big or expensive— consider a sleep-in, a new magazine, a coffee at your favorite café, or a night at the movies.

I used to look at tasks in one big chunk and I would avoid them at all costs. It's now a lot easier to do something when I break it down into smaller parts.

— EVANGELINE, 23, STUDENT

When I am procrastinating I write a list of what needs to be done and sort it by urgency and deadline. I do all the small tasks first to give me a sense of achievement. This makes the rest seem much less daunting and overwhelming.

— TRACEY, 31, WEB DESIGNER

Action task: Use a four-column chart to overcome your procrastination. In the first column list the issue, then the reason you are procrastinating, the options for the solution and the action you are committed to taking. This technique allows you to identify what is blocking you and helps you to move forward rather than reaching a dead end. Next time you find yourself stuck, use this four-point plan to get back on track.

Extend your comfort zone

How many times have you heard Susan Jeffer's slogan "Feel the fear and do it anyway"? Jeffer is renowned for her comment that "Pushing through fear is less frightening than living with the underlying fear that comes from a feeling of helplessness."

Maybe you felt the fear and pushed yourself outside your comfort zone when you learned to water-ski, did a bungee jump or even stood up at a meeting to speak? Instead of letting nerves overcome you, meet challenges head-on with excitement. I often turn my nervousness into positive enthusiasm by calling on the mind-body techniques discussed in Chapter 4. In hindsight I often find that my worry is unfounded, and by then I have extended my comfort zone, making a new benchmark for my confidence. In this way, extending your comfort zone will stretch your achievements. We are all intrinsically capable of so much more than we think. Time and time again clients report back to me that something they were anxious about doing didn't turn out to be that bad after all. Imagine that! Our minds really do work in mysterious ways. Push yourself just a bit further each and every time you do something, whether it's running an extra mile or doing a little something extra for someone.

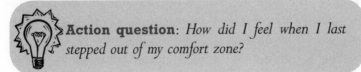

Action question: *How did I feel when I last stepped out of my comfort zone?*

You may need a boost of positive thinking (see Chapter 4) and confidence to overcome your doubts and fears. This is especially true if you have always chosen the easy and comfortable way instead of challenging yourself. Having a little adventure in your life doesn't have to mean death-defying acts. It can mean personally challenging yourself to compete in a fun triathlon, volunteer for a charity or try anything new.

Action task: Analyze your personal priorities and goals and identify at least five ways in which you can extend your comfort zone. Then challenge yourself!

Persevere and make every day count

Call it persistence, determination, doggedness, diligence, sheer willpower or strength. You will certainly need doses of these qualities to reach your aspirations and achieve work/life balance. Your ideal life won't just materialize overnight; there is a direct correlation between your efforts and the results you will gain.

Not long ago I met a particularly inspiring young performer who was working toward a major international audition. With a full year ahead of her to plan and prepare, Kelly (20) took the approach of "making every day count." She had an amazing opportunity to audition and she wanted to ensure she was in the best possible position to be successful, otherwise another year would pass before she would be eligible to audition again. To help manage herself in the lead-up she decided she would ask herself at the end of each day if she had made it count, by practicing her singing, dancing, acting and self-care. This meant that every single day she was taking small action steps toward her big dream.

We can all use this approach to ensure our own success and balance in life. In the way that 12-step recovery programs focus on one day at a time, making every day count can make an overwhelming goal, like Kelly's, much more manageable.

Are you working toward a promotion? Raising a family? Fitness training? Looking for a new relationship? Ask yourself, "What can I do today to make a difference?" If you veer off course for a day, this makes it much easier to get back on track and make the next day valuable in your progress.

Use this daily review to monitor your progress:

- What did I accomplish today toward my goals?
- What did I not achieve today that I said I would?
- What obstacles or barriers are in my way for tomorrow?
- What options are available to me for tomorrow?
- What action steps will I take tomorrow?

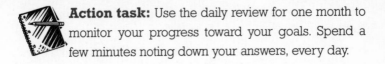 **Action task:** Use the daily review for one month to monitor your progress toward your goals. Spend a few minutes noting down your answers, every day.

One thing I never forget is that hard jobs never take as long as you think.
— DAVID, 58, HEALTH CONSULTANT

Seek feedback to continually improve

Effective feedback can accelerate your learning, and inspire, motivate and encourage action. It takes courage to step outside your comfort zone and ask for feedback, but it's a beneficial process that will ultimately improve your performance.

Feedback is basically useful information that is passed back to someone to help them assess their performance. You may already be helping others with useful feedback. Have you ever reviewed an assignment for a friend or been asked for advice on a colleague's work proposal? A smart tip to remember when providing feedback is to sandwich a suggestion for improvement between two positive and encouraging comments. Toastmasters International, which uses this technique, calls it CRC: that is, "commend, recommend, commend."

Always balance difficult messages with positive statements.

Feedback is often confused with its evil opposite—criticism. The difference is that effective feedback is given in a positive way, and is based on fact rather than opinion, is beneficial and constructive. Good feedback needs to be clear and specific so it can be used toward a solution to an issue.

Earlier in my career as a journalist, I learned a good lesson about receiving feedback. It's so easy to take negative comments to heart, but my first lesson showed me how feedback improved the quality of my work tenfold. I distinctly remember completing my first article for a weekly magazine with trepidation. I was so apprehensive I almost didn't want to place it on the editor's desk! Seeing my first story marked up in red pen could have been devastating, but the suggested amendments improved the article markedly. The value of having fresh and experienced eyes review my work meant the story was dramatically improved. I now look forward to feedback to improve the quality of my writing, rather than worrying about how many suggested changes there may be.

Whatever your field, always listen and be grateful for feedback—whether you are taking up public speaking, learning to cook or to dance, starting a new job or parenting. In fact, most work/life balance goals can benefit from feedback to facilitate your continual improvement.

Start by finding a mentor, role model or peer who you can approach for feedback. Open the conversation by explaining what you would like feedback on, in general terms, perhaps relating to a specific goal. Once your supporter has agreed to engage in feedback, here are a few questions you can use to get the best results:

- What are my positive strengths (in relation to my goal or performance)?
- What else do I do well?
- What can I do differently or improve?
- What could I continue doing?

- What could I stop doing?
- What can I start doing?

Receive feedback graciously (at least say "Thank you") and don't contradict the other person's view. Listen carefully to the feedback you receive and then acknowledge the opportunity for change. After a session of feedback ask yourself, "What did I learn about myself and what will I now do differently as a result of that conversation?"

Action task: Choose someone you admire and trust, and approach them with a request to discuss your performance. Tell them the specific area you require feedback on, and use appropriate questions to gain this information. Then on your own, using this information as a starting point, choose at least two changes you are prepared to make to improve your performance and move you closer to your goals.

Change the things you can

As you progress toward your ideal life you will need to evaluate what is working, what isn't working and where you need to make changes and modify your action plans for the best results. First, focus on what is working in your action plan. Don't be tempted to spend time and energy on low-yield plans. It will soon be obvious if what you are doing isn't working, and if this happens take a new approach and try something else. Then, evaluate if this new approach is working. If you feel truly stuck just do something different—anything to help you move forward to a better outcome.

> **Hot tip:** *If you can't change a situation, change your attitude and get positive!*

The best way to make changes is to monitor your progress. Regularly reviewing your goals can help you focus your time and energy on what is most important to you. In *Aspirations* I introduced this evaluation technique that you can use to maximize your motivation to make changes in life. Use this checklist to measure your progress with your own action plans:

- What have I accomplished this week/month toward my goals?
- What did I not achieve that I said I would?
- What challenges or potential obstacles am I now facing?
- What options are available to me to move myself another step toward my goals?
- Of these options, which action do I plan to take?
- How am I going to ensure I take this action?
- What extra support do I need to succeed with these plans?

 Action task: For 12 consecutive weeks use the weekly evaluation checklist to track your progress and assist you in modifying your action plans.

I gain a huge sense of relief when I ditch something after realizing that it is not worth pursuing after all.

— DEBBIE, 38, ADMINISTRATOR

Go for gold

Why be average or good when you can be great, fabulous and your personal best? Going for gold is exactly this: striving for personal excellence. It is about taking your goals to the next level by holding yourself accountable. In this section, I investigate how important emotional intelligence is in creating balance, along with consistency and commitment, plus a few extra strategies that will soon have you lifting your game and realizing your potential in every way.

Be accountable

Whether you are accountable to a coach, mentor, friend or *Stop Living Your Job, Start Living Your Life* motivational group, you need to be fully accountable to yourself first.

In seminar workshops I often present groups with this sample personal contract to cement their commitment to success. It is often met with mixed views. Regardless, I find that the participants who write some kind of contract holding themselves accountable succeed in their goals far more often than those who don't.

Sample personal contract:

I .... take personal responsibility for transforming my life. I am willing to experiment with changing my behavior, trying new tools and techniques, reassessing the self-beliefs I hold, setting effective goals to stretch my comfort zone, and removing sources of stress in my life as I redesign the way I approach my life. I agree to complete each action step honestly and

to the best of my ability and take immediate and positive
action on the plans I write.

Sign here..

Date...

Action task: Complete this personal contract or
customize your own to reflect your work/life balance
goals. Place your contract where you will see it every
day, as a visual reminder of your intentions.

Be consistent

Studies suggest that it takes 21 consecutive days to form a new
habit after making a change. Being reliable and steady may
sound like boring qualities, but being consistent will increase
your effectiveness and performance at home and at work.

Often the first flush of enthusiasm for our life changes
can be diluted as we encounter challenges and setbacks.
We have already discussed perseverance as a strategy, along
with making every day count. Just as I suggested taking
a first, manageable step, resolve to keep taking consistent
bite-sized steps in the right direction. By doing this, you
will find that in less than a month the changes you have
made will become new work/life balance habits.

Paula (53) came to coaching realizing that a year had
passed without her making any progress toward a specific
project goal. She had an exciting entrepreneurial idea that
she wanted to research fully and analyze for feasibility
before committing further time, money and effort.
Together we put in place a workable plan that saw weekly
actions take her step by step closer to her goal. This is a
simple yet effective approach to being consistent. If Paula

had launched headlong into all of the possible action tasks at once, she would have made progress with some and not others. She would have settled back into her regular routine, dismissing her "failure" by saying she "gave it a shot." Her consistent actions soon paid off and she launched an innovative business which was a key focus in helping her achieve work/life balance.

Make the changes last

Change isn't easy, but it is an important factor in our lives. Even when change is for all the right reasons, like work/life balance and healthy living, it can still be challenging. It is important to understand the process of change as we make adjustments to our lives to achieve the balance we desire.

There are many theories on change as it is a very complex issue. A widely accepted theory is the Stages of Change model from behavioral psychologist James Prochaska. He identified the following five key stages:

1. Pre-contemplation: not yet considering change, maybe unaware of need.
2. Contemplation: considering change, but lack solid plans.
3. Preparation: planning to take action.
4. Action: completing the task.
5. Maintenance: continuing to take action with results.

This model shows there are five stages everyone goes through to change. While each step is important, the preparation step is pivotal as it involves setting goals (see Chapter

1) and making action plans. There is a sixth stage that is often used in this model—relapse, when you can temporarily slip back into your old ways. Often people who are trying to change health habits such as stopping smoking can find themselves in this relapse phase. Being in relapse doesn't mean you are a total failure; it is a normal part of change. At this stage, however, don't give up totally: stop and evaluate what worked, what didn't work, and how you can commence the process again and achieve better results. Working through the process systematically will ensure lasting changes are made as you think about what you are doing and what the resulting improvements will ultimately mean in your life.

It is often said that the only constant in life is change. Think of all the changes you have already experienced, from leaving school, starting or leaving a job, beginning and ending relationships, moving house or becoming a parent. Change is a natural process we encounter at all stages of our life cycle. Review the last five years of your life and consider your major life changes.

Action task: Determine which stage of change you are at with your work/life balance goals. Acknowledge your efforts to date and strive for the next step! If you do find yourself in relapse, look for additional support and use the strategies on accountability to assist you.

Be emotionally intelligent

The concept of emotional intelligence was introduced in 1995 by Daniel Goleman in his ground-breaking book *Emotional Intelligence*. According to Goleman, our emotional aptitude determines how well we can use the other skills we possess, including our intellect. His theory is important in understanding why one person reaches the heights of success while another of the same intellect does not.

As a concept, emotional intelligence is growing in popularity and finding a niche in the workplace. Goleman suggests that you can test for EQ in a similar way to an IQ test. Possessing emotional intelligence includes self-awareness, self-control, motivation, empathy and social skills. In summary, EQ is the ability to manage your feelings and thoughts. An important component is also being able to read the moods of others and respond in the best way.

You can develop your emotional intelligence by recognizing and learning from your emotions and being empathetic to others. If you can manage your thoughts, feelings and emotions, you will then be well positioned to focus on your priorities, and to communicate with others more productively.

Stay committed

Many people have great ideas but abandon them when they begin to need commitment. Consider how many dreams you have not yet achieved because you are lacking the commitment. Commitment is being able to do whatever needs to be done to make your dream come true. If, for example, you want to be financially free in 10 years' time, you will need strong commitment to a budget and financial plan, starting today.

Hot tip: *Always ask yourself, "How committed am I to achieving this goal?"*

Being committed is doing what you say you are going to do, or carrying out your intentions. It is not essentially about your obligations to others; rather, your commitment to yourself and your life plan. Don't just pay lip service to your personal priorities. If you have thought about making a change in your life, generate some kind of ownership and responsibility that will ensure you are fully committed.

I regularly see clients in our coaching practice who want to decrease their work hours but lack the commitment to make the change. Commitment to a goal like this is worthless if you don't recognize why leaving work at 6 p.m. is important. You need to look at the consequences of not being committed to your goal, and what your life will be like when the goal is achieved. The reason you need high levels of commitment to make changes in your life is that low commitment will result in other priorities overriding your goals. Using the work hours example again, if you have low commitment, work requests will easily seem more important than being at home.

When you consider the concept of the "path of least resistance," you can appreciate why commitment wanes so quickly. It is a lot easier to continue doing what you have always done than to challenge yourself to extend your comfort zone and modify your behavior to get the results you want.

Hot tip: *Increase your commitment by visualizing how you will feel when you have succeeded.*

Incorporate mind-body techniques (as discussed in Chapter 4) such as affirmations, meditation and visualization to help increase your commitment levels. And use these self-coaching questions to determine how committed you are to taking action toward achieving your aspirations:

- How exciting, energizing and inspiring does my goal feel?
- Am I able to invest the money, time and energy needed?
- What is my intuition telling me about my level of commitment?
- How will my life be different when I have achieved this goal?
- How does this goal fit with my overall work/life balance vision?

Hot tip: *To monitor your commitment, rate each of your goals with a commitment level on a scale of 1 to 10, where 1 is uncommitted and 10 is fully committed. The lower your rating, the more commitment you will need to gather to realize your goal.*

Action task: Review each of your goals and give yourself a commitment rating on a scale of 1 to 10. If you don't have a commitment level of 7, 8, 9 or 10 ask yourself what needs to be different to increase your commitment?

Celebrate success

When was the last time you celebrated a life transition like graduating, getting a new job or moving to a new town? My research shows that 81% of survey respondents do celebrate their achievements but surprisingly, 14% of respondents don't celebrate at all and 5% simply plan their next goal.

If we set compelling goals, evaluate our progress and modify our actions, we should have many more occasions to celebrate success. It is important to take credit for the hard work and effort we have put in. I encourage clients and friends alike to celebrate each forward movement as they satisfy their goals. Celebrating success doesn't mean you have to show off with a fancy party; there are plenty of simple ways to recognize your achievement. Half of my survey respondents said they share their celebrations with their partner, family or friends. After dinner or drinks with family, the most popular ideas include vacations, shopping, a glass of wine, buying new clothes, chocolate, having a massage, seeing a movie, a new hairdo and devouring an ice cream.

Enjoy the rewards of success as a time when your dreams connect to your reality. How satisfying is it to complete a qualification, begin a new relationship or finish the marathon you have been training for? Consider how you can celebrate passing a test, gaining a driver's license, managing a stressful time, graduating, winning a promotion or recovering from illness.

> *I simply give myself a pat on the back and think,*
> *"Good for me."*
> — ANDREA, 50, RECEPTIONIST

Record your accomplishment so that when you are striving for another goal in life you have a benchmark that shows you really can do it when the going gets tough. It's more likely you will believe in your ability to meet other goals in the future if you take the time to reflect on your achievements.

As a guideline, make sure your rewards are relevant and tailored to a specific activity and time. For example, a king-size chocolate bar may not be the best reward for finally starting a fitness program! Consider instead a therapeutic massage for meeting certain time-specific fitness goals. If you have set a goal of leaving work at 6 p.m. every night, perhaps celebrate with a special dinner with your family on Friday. To keep motivated week to week, maybe treat yourself with small rewards. Or as you reach milestones, celebrate in a way that acknowledges your achievement.

Recognize and reward the success of others, too—acknowledging success both at home and at work helps to refine life balance. Celebrate with your partner, family and friends so they feel involved in your achievements and understand how much satisfaction and value you have gained from the experience.

One danger of goal-setting and focusing on your big-picture aspirations is that you can feel you are caught up in the future. Celebrating success draws you firmly into the present by letting you enjoy the journey.

I firmly believe that to be fully alive you need to embrace experiences through celebrations. This can be a natural extension of regular family events like birthdays and anniversaries. Celebrating success is very motivating. Remember that celebrating success is more than an event, it's a way of building a positive attitude in life. So often we criticize ourselves or let those negative, limiting beliefs stop us from achieving what we are capable of.

Celebrating success reinforces our much-needed positive beliefs. When working with clients I find this strategy reinforces their self-belief before they embark on their next goal. I have seen very clear results and increased confidence which have propelled clients to keep moving forward in life.

> *Firstly, the feeling of completion is very rewarding. Then I celebrate with a lunch or get-together with friends to announce that I have completed another step in my plan.*
>
> — ELAINE, 55, EDUCATOR

Action task: Choose ways to celebrate your success, both the small daily steps and your end goal. Start by writing a list of 15–20 possibilities for personal rewards. Factor these rewards into your goal-setting plans.

Get going: chapter summary

Go for it!
- Take the first step
- Fake it till you make it
- Brand yourself
- Be natural and enthusiastic
- Be flexible

Go hard

- Maintain momentum
- Overcome procrastination
- Extend your comfort zone
- Persevere and make every day count
- Seek feedback to continually improve
- Change the things you can

Go for gold

- Be accountable
- Be consistent
- Make the changes last
- Be emotionally intelligent
- Stay committed
- Celebrate success.

Conclusion

*If you do what you have always done, you will get
what you have always got.*
— DAVID TAYLOR

Some time ago when I was in the greenroom at a TV studio
waiting to be interviewed, I met the manager of a music
band. We got chatting and he gave me a fabulous analogy—
that life is like a pizza. Seriously! If you want to eat a
gourmet pizza, you need to decide what toppings you
want, place an order and then either collect it or wait for
the delivery. A pizza won't just materialize out of thin air
when you are hungry. Similarly, it is highly unlikely that
you will wake up tomorrow morning to a perfectly
balanced life. Life is like buying a pizza in that you have to
decide what you want and go after it with determination.

Each of the strategies in this book relies totally on one
person—you! Living a balanced life won't happen until you
commit to taking the necessary action steps. To lead
a fulfilling life you need first to understand yourself and
increase your self-awareness. By doing this you can focus on
your dreams and priorities, ensuring you do things that give
meaning (and balance!) to your life. Use the strategies
discussed in Chapter 2 to help you organize and manage

your daily life. This will free up your time and energy to focus on the big picture and regain the balance you are searching for.

To achieve work/life balance you also need to actively manage stress and choose healthy living. The mind-body strategies introduced in Chapter 4 will also help you manage stress and rebalance your life. Lastly, use the strategies in Chapter 5 to accelerate your progress and make your improvements last.

Let's recap on each of the strategies to help you achieve work/life balance:

Chapter 1: Get focused

Focus on your dreams

- Think big
- Find your passion
- Create your vision
- Turn the dream into reality
- Prioritize your goals

Focus on your priorities

- Discover your purpose
- Live your values
- Find work you love

Focus on people

- Build a strong network of family and friends
- Look to role models
- Use a mentor
- Start coaching
- Create your own *Stop Living Your Job, Start Living Your Life* motivational group
- Network formally

Focus on financial freedom
- Pursue your dreams
- Set financial goals and make a plan
- Change your beliefs about money
- Find opportunities for generating passive income
- Think long term
- Take control of your finances.

Chapter 2: Get organized

Organize your time

- Minimize time-traps
- Track your time
- Plan a realistic schedule
- Manage phone use
- Set boundaries for quiet time
- Tune into your body clock
- Trade time

Organize your daily life

- Use technology to your advantage
- Manage paper flow
- Prepare ahead of time
- Delegate
- Schedule for spontaneity and interruptions
- Make it a date!
- Be smart and multitask

Organize your space

- Clear clutter
- Put systems in place
- Have a home for everything

Organize your finances
- Establish your reality
- Be brave and budget
- Cut luxuries to save
- Automate
- Reduce debt
- Learn to negotiate

Organize your career
- Redesign your work
- Start your own business.

Chapter 3: Don't get stressed

Stress identification
- Understand stress
- Look for your personal stress triggers

Stress management
- Eliminate it!
- Say "No"!
- Create time to slow down
- Pamper yourself

Stress and health
- Eat better
- Exercise more
- Sleep well.

Chapter 4: Get connected

Connect with your aspirations
- Visualize your success
- Trust your intuition

Connect with your words
- Use affirmations
- Mind your language
- Write a journal
- Write a work/life balance statement

Connect with your creativity
- Be inspired
- Shake up your routine
- Write yourself creative
- Keep a creative scrapbook

Connect with your thoughts
- Listen to yourself
- Believe in yourself
- Adopt a positive attitude
- Meditate.

Chapter 5: Get going

Go for it!
- Take the first step
- Fake it till you make it
- Brand yourself
- Be natural and enthusiastic
- Be flexible

Go hard
- Maintain momentum
- Overcome procrastination
- Extend your comfort zone
- Persevere and make every day count
- Seek feedback to continually improve
- Change the things you can

Go for gold

- Be accountable
- Be consistent
- Make the changes last
- Be emotionally intelligent
- Stay committed
- Celebrate success.

Just as the last strategy in this book has encouraged you to celebrate success, I would like to do exactly that with you! Please email me your success stories via our website—www.aspirationscoaching.com—highlighting which strategies work best for you and outlining any additional strategies of your own that you would like to share.

Maintaining balance is the key to both professional and personal success. Always be sure about what you want, plan and prepare, live a healthy life, stay motivated and always celebrate success. Enjoy and good luck!

Further reading

Berman Fortgang, Laura, *Take Yourself to the Top*, Thorsons, 1999

Burns, Rebeckh, & van der Fluit, Peter, *Thought Miracles: Affirmations to Ignite Your Future*, Thorsons, 2002

Butler-Bowdon, Tom, *50 Self Help Classics: Books to Change Your Life*, Simon & Schuster, 2001

Harrold, Fiona, *The 10-Minute Life Coach*, Hodder and Stoughton, 2002

Harvard Business Review on Work and Life Balance, Harvard Business School Press, 2000

Henderson, Michael, *Finding True North*, HarperBusiness, 2003

Merrill, Roger A. & Merrill, Rebecca R., *Life Matters*, McGraw Hill, 2003

Morgenstern, Julie, *Time Management from the Inside Out*, Hodderand Stoughton, 2000

Richardson, Cheryl, *Stand Up for Your Life*, Free Press, 2002

Spillane, Mary, *Branding Yourself: How to Look, Sound and Behave Your Way to Success*, Pan, 2000

Stuart, Susanna, *Your Family Fortune*, Random House, 2002

Whitmore, John, *Coaching for Performance*, Nicholas Brealey Publishing, 1992

Other Ulysses Press books

A Girl's Guide to Money: Make the Rent, Control Your Credit Cards, Afford a Car, Pay Your Cell Bill and Still Have Money for Shopping Sprees and Nights on the Town
Laura Brady, $12.95

This full-color guide presents indispensible financial advice on bank accounts, budgeting, avoiding and managing debt, and much more.

Fit in 15: 15-Minute Morning Workouts That Balance Cardio, Strength and Flexibility
Steven Stiefel, $12.95

The *Fit in 15* program varies 15-minute workouts on different days of the week in order to develop all elements of a healthy body, including muscle building, core strengthening, fat burning and more.

Flip the Switch: 40 Anytime, Anywhere Meditations in 5 Minutes or Less
Eric Harrison, $10.95

Flip the Switch points out the time gaps that come throughout the day (idling at a red light, waiting for a computer to restart, standing in line at the grocery store) and teaches specially designed meditations that fit each of these situations.

1001 Little Health Miracles: Shortcuts to Feeling Good, Looking Great and Living Healthy
Esme Floyd, $12.95

Packed with head-to-toe tips on topics ranging from nutrition and fitness to healing and wellness, *1001 Little Health Miracles* serves up a vast array of simple solutions that provides huge health benefits.

Music of Silence: A Sacred Journey
through the Hours of the Day
David Steindl-Rast with Sharon Lebell
Introduction by Kathleen Norris, $12.00

A noted Benedictine monk shows us how to incorporate the sacred meaning of monastic life into our everyday world by paying attention to the "seasons of the day" and the enlivening messages to be found in each moment.

What Would Buddha Do?:
101 Answers to Life's Daily Dilemmas
Franz Metcalf, $9.95

Much as the "WWJD?" books help Christians live better lives by drawing on the wisdom of Jesus, this "WWBD?" book provides advice on improving your life by following the wisdom of another great teacher—Buddha.

To order these books call 800-377-2542 or 510-601-8301, fax 510-601-8307, e-mail ulysses@ulyssespress.com, or write to Ulysses Press, P.O. Box 3440, Berkeley, CA 94703. All retail orders are shipped free of charge. California residents must include sales tax. Allow two to three weeks for delivery.

About the author

Andrea Molloy is a founding director of Aspirations Ltd., which offers both personal and corporate coaching services, customized workshops and seminars. Clients include Coca-Cola Amatil NZ Ltd., the New Zealand Rugby Union, Lion Nathan and Telecom NZ. Andrea is trained and accredited by the Life Coaching Academy and is a member of the ICF. She was president of the Auckland chapter of the ICF in 2003. Andrea is a regular TV and radio guest, and writes motivational articles for magazines. She also holds a degree in sociology from Victoria University of Wellington. Her first book, *Aspirations: 8 Easy Steps to Coach Yourself to Success*, was published by Random House (NZ) Ltd. in 2003. For personal and corporate coaching services Andrea can be contacted via:

www.aspirationscoaching.com

Register online for a FREE monthly self-coaching newsletter. Andrea welcomes your feedback. Answer her questionnaire about *Stop Living Your Job, Start Living Your Life* on the website.

Further information

The International Coach Federation (ICF) is the worldwide professional organization for coaches. As an independent body it sets out codes of conduct and ethical guidelines for the profession: www.coachfederation.org